| square
circle
star
triangle | Discover your Shape to shape your world |

G000160667

.the
shapes
test™

UNDERSTAND YOURSELF
UNDERSTAND OTHERS
MAKE YOURSELF UNDERSTOOD

PAUL CLAYTON GIBBS

Harris
House
Publishing

MyShapes Journal
Copyright © 2021 by Paul Clayton Gibbs

Published by Harris House Publishing
harrishousepublishing.com
Colleyville, Texas
USA

This title is available in other formats.
978-1-946369-53-6
978-1-946369-54-3

Cover creation by Ronaldo Andrade, Jr. | design by Paul Clayton Gibbs

What people are saying about The Shapes Test™

THE SPOUSE
"Our cultures and family dynamics couldn't be more opposite! This book lets me understand my husband's frame of mind and be more supportive in his endeavors."

Alexandra Swires-Murphy | Syria | Triangle
An Arab married to an American

THE BUSINESS CEO
"Most of my time is spent navigating people's challenges. The Shapes Test™ has created a powerful tool with which to overcome them."

Matthew Powell | USA | Star
CEO of Dallas company Moroch Partners

THE RECRUITMENT MANAGER
"It's clear to me that integrating the Shapes Test™ into any hiring process will help you identify what makes a candidate tick and will unearth what motivates their talent."

Ian Peacock | England | Triangle
Hiring and Talent specialist in the innovation-led technology sector

THE SENIOR VICE PRINCIPAL
"This book is very powerful, it is more than a diagnostic test. It has helped me grasp why some staff run with an idea, whilst others question or retaliate."

Kirsty Sturdy | England | Circle
Senior Vice-Principal of a large secondary academy in England

THE PARENT OF A BLENDED FAMILY
"It helps me get the whole family moving in the same direction, and with the same language, even if family members are moving at different speeds."

Mike Sherrill | USA | Circle
Parent of seven children

THE SCHOOL CHAPLAIN
"The Shapes Test™ is beneficial as a tool to reinforce the identity of the students we work with and helps prepare them for future success and achievement."

Gary Ward | Australia | Triangle
Chaplain of Alta-1 CARE School

THE LAW STUDENT
"As a student of Law and Criminology, it is incredibly useful when advocating on someone else's behalf, forming and maintaining a level of trust with potential clients."

Daniel Jeffries |England | Triangle
Student of Law and Criminology LLB

THE NGO DIRECTOR
"The author seems to understand how different Shapes feel. If the fire in your heart and mind needs to be stirred, this excellent book is for you!"

Sakhawat Masih | Pakistan | Circle
Award-winning Director of The Servant Project, a nationwide Relief Agency

THE VOCATIONAL TRAINER
"Simple and grabbable from the outset, yet incisively far-reaching. A must-have for anyone intentionally discovering why they are here!"

Andy Flaherty | Australia | Star
Outdoor Guide and Team Building Facilitator

THE CHURCH MINISTER
"It will help staff and volunteers in our church cooperate, resolve conflict, and create solutions as we integrate these principles into our ministry."

Leonard Browning | USA | Star
Senior Pastor of The Journey Church Colorado

THE BUSINESS GRADUATE
"I'm already incorporating the language I've learned to express myself and I have noticed a significant difference in my relationships."

Isabella Scarinzi | Brasil | Square
Business and Marketing major at Oklahoma Baptist University

Thank you for purchasing this journal!

By doing so you are contributing to the work of our partners across the globe as we train young people in how to build healthy relationships using The Shapes Test™.

Today, young people are struggling with issues that are being highlighted with the breakdown of the family unit and an increasingly polarized world. This leaves many young people without the help and input of a nurturing community. Many children, teens, and young adults feel alone and unable to cope with the pressures of daily life. This leads to an increase in:

Suicide.
Mental health issues.
Drug and alcohol abuse.
Relational insecurities.
Isolation.
Hopelessness.
Debilitating fear.

Our response to these problems is to work with our partners to provide mentors for young people. These mentors work alongside schools, youth agencies, faith communities, and neighborhood projects worldwide. They help young people build their confidence in who they are and their ability to relate to the world around them.

Support is raised for these projects through the sales of The Shapes Test™ book and MyShapes companion journal, the Masterclass Training events we present, and the other forms of training that The Shapes Test™ provides. The material within this book is copyrighted for that purpose and we appreciate your respect of that.

We do not believe that young people need to be victims but instead can be a positive force in our world. We believe in them and want to help them believe in themselves! Please understand that you are now part of that process and you can follow that work on our social media platforms.

Let's build something good together!

Discover your 'Shape-Weight'

Just exactly how much of a 'Square' or 'Triangle' are you?
What is the order of your other Shapes?
What percentage of each one do you possess?
You can now take the test and get answers to all these questions!

Discovering your
'Shape-Weight' will help you
understand your personality
type to a much greater degree
and figure out why sometimes
your primary Shape does not
quite fit you. It will create the
opportunity for greater
discussions with your friends,
and of course allow others to
better understand who you
are!

Go online to find out more at:
theshapestest.com

Get Training!

The Shapes Test™ offers fun, interactive presentations to help people build something good together. A Masterclass can be shaped to your needs in both length and content, and we have multiple formats for various settings.

Masterclasses are available for your business, organization, church, school or neighborhood event and come in various formats both in-person and online.

Go online to find out more at:
theshapestest.com

Contents

1. Crimewatch

How can we build something good together?

RQ

Why?

I knew I had a problem when the police telephoned me late one night to ask:

"Mr. Gibbs, do you know a Miss Joanne Adamson?"

I told the officer I did, explaining that she was on the team of community workers that I was managing in my hometown of Manchester, England.

"Mr. Gibbs, can I also ask if you know a Mr. Gary Ward?"

Certainly! Gary was on the same team. He was a local lad in his twenties, fun-loving with a great sense of humor. Joanne was a little younger and from the south of the country, which made her . . . in our eyes at least . . . a little 'posh.' Therefore, Gary used to tease her in that particularly Northern English way, where you mess with someone because you care about them, not because you don't.

I thought Joanne understood this. Apparently, I was wrong . . .

"Mr. Gibbs, after tonight's television episode of *Crimewatch UK*,[1] Miss Adamson called into the police response center, claiming that Mr. Ward perfectly fits the description of the serial killer we are currently seeking to track down. Can you please help us with our enquiries?"

Now, that's a personality clash!

Note that I said personality clash, not character clash. Both Joanne and Gary had excellent character. They were honest, authentic, faithful, and caring people. Both had volunteered a year of their lives to sacrificially serve young people, mentoring and inspiring them to be the best that they could be. However, Joanne struggled not only to understand why her colleague was doing the things he did, but also how she could effectively communicate to him that she did not like it. Gary, on the other hand, was completely oblivious to the fact there was even a problem!

After some time spent assuring the police officer that Gary was not their man, I spoke to Joanne the following morning. I asked her if she really believed that her fellow team member could have been the person wanted for the stalking, attacking, and killing of innocent women. I found her answer interesting. With all the sweetness of a British 'Southern belle,' she replied:

> "Well, I just thought he might be. After all, you have to go with your gut instinct, don't you?"

Well, no, actually, you don't.

In fact, our gut instinct can be quite problematic when it comes to judging others. According to The Innocence Project, nearly 78% of criminal exonerations are directly associated with mistaken eyewitness identification due to 'intuitive judgments.'[2]

Is there a better way?

Gary and Joanne were part of the first team I recruited in the early nineties, but they would not be the only good people who would suffer from a bad relationship. Twenty-five years, and thousands of team members later, I like to think I'm getting a little better at spotting and resolving these problems . . . not just professionally, but personally. However, during that time, the world has become even more polarized. Relational intelligence seems to be on the decline. The ability to converse, collaborate, and cope with the inevitable stresses and conflicts in everyday relationships appears to be disintegrating. This leads people to constrict their friendship groups and withdraw into their own echo chambers. In fact, in reply to the question, "What's the biggest problem in the world today?", the Nobel Peace Prize-winning nun, Mother Teresa said:

> "The biggest problem in the world today is that we draw the circle [around us] too small."[3]

I want us to build something good together, and so, several years ago, I began to ask, how can I reverse this negative process . . . at least with those upon whom I have some influence? Perhaps along with Joanne, Gary, and myself, you also have similar questions . . .

Why can't we all just get along?

Why do people behave the way they do?

Why don't people understand me?

My desire is to find a way for everyone to understand everyone else a little bit better. This may help us more intentionally and thoughtfully communicate, forgive, love, care, motivate, and challenge each other so that we can all become the best version of ourselves.

Like you, I hope to make the world a better place.

How?

First, let me clearly state that I am not an academic; I am a practitioner.

My primary job is not to write books, but to empower people. I lead an organization that recruits volunteers, mainly young adults. We train and place them into teams that work together for the common good. They build working relationships between individuals in various community groups, schools, agencies, churches, and businesses.

Many travel overseas for a minimum of one year. This means I am responsible for teams of mixed races, cultures, and languages on six continents. Interestingly, the leadership guru John Maxwell describes young people and volunteers as two of the most challenging categories of folk to lead.[4] Although The Shapes Test™ builds upon previous scientific work (see Appendix 2), if you are looking for an academic and primarily theoretical book, then it is likely you will find better material elsewhere. However, if you are on the hunt for a practical guide to better understand yourself and others, then I think I can help.

For that purpose, this book unpacks a personality inventory, plus tried-and-tested ideas.

It is written for the average person looking for practical tips to improve the way they shape the relationships around them. Personality tests have been popularized with many variations on social media. In fact, there seems to be no end to them! Perhaps, like me, you engaged with one or two for fun. Maybe you also now know what breed of dog best reflects your attitude to life, which city you really should have been born in, and which Lord of the Rings character encapsulates your greatest strength. However, like me, you also may have discovered that identifying which Disney Princess[5] you are does not bring you the lasting inner peace and life purpose you might have imagined. Of course, few take these pseudo-scientific tests seriously. However, they do reveal two desires all of us possess when it comes to relationships:

To understand ourselves better and to be better understood by others.

Although the concept of four temperaments was originally discovered in Ancient Greece, some would argue that it was not until September 2018 that scientific studies finally confirmed their existence.[6] However, books, websites, consultants, and magazines have promoted them for a long time because, to a degree, the proof was already in the pudding. Over the years, I have used various personality appraisals in my work and personal life, and yet I found that individually they lacked the essential ingredients I was looking for to achieve my goal. Before I explain what I believe The Shapes Test™ does that is somewhat different, let me unpack the personality tests I have used in the past.

Myers-Briggs

The most comprehensive 'personality inventory' I know is the Myers-Briggs Type Indicator (MBTI). It is thorough, meticulous, academic, and comprehensive. In my eyes, it is the Rolls-Royce of personality tests, and I would recommend it if your primary goal is to simply get to know yourself a little better. In my experience, however, it does not lend itself to everyday conversation, because people's results are not easy to remember. When someone tells me their MBTI type, a string of four letters representing one of sixteen possibilities, I invariably have to ask them to remind me of its meaning.

StrengthsFinder (CliftonStrengths)

I have used people's StrengthsFinder reports in mentoring situations to great effect, and I love the author's tone when explaining the results. It is excellent in helping people figure out how to best use their talents and gifts, particularly in a work setting. If you are looking for a great tool to discover what makes you great, you might want to check it out. However, its specificity makes it too limiting for my purpose.

Love Languages

This is another wonderful example of research leveraged to help relationships, particularly in the way one gives and receives love or appreciation. I am sure it has helped deepen many relationships around the world. Yet, my desire is to present something more holistic that encompasses a much fuller picture of personality types and provides all the tools necessary to build something good together.

True Colors

> For some time, the most helpful personality test I found was True Colors. It had the simplicity I was looking for, and it is a good tool to help others express themselves. However, it lacks some of the depth and width of the pragmatic takeaways that I am looking to provide. Plus, the idea of categorizing one personality type as the 'Feeling' child and another as the 'Thinking' child does not sit well with me because neither intellect nor compassion are tied to personality. I have also found that colors are not as good of a visual metaphor as shapes, which lend themselves to further interpretation by those participating in a conversation or discussion.

All of the above are excellent tools. Some of them are purposely complex or intentionally simple. Most of them have very specific objectives. Yet, I needed something unique to unite people. The Shapes Test™ is the result of rethinking and improving upon what I previously found helpful. In an appendix at the end of this book, I briefly outline how it was created. During the last number of years, I have used the material not just within our own organization, but throughout the communities we reach. On six continents, this more holistic approach has allowed us to move much closer to our goal of building global friendships, teams, and partnerships.

Essentially, it aims to provide a one-size-fits-all solution to fulfill the following objectives:

Identifiable

> The Shapes Test™ provides an alternative way to identify motives. The benefit here is that they tend to limit knee-jerk 'go-to' reactions such as: "They did that because they're a bad person," or "They suggested that because they are not on my side." Instead, the ability to recognize someone's Shape produces a more understanding dynamic and a different perspective of why people behave the way they do.

Shareable

One of my five keys to building culture is having a common language. More than any tool I have previously used, The Shapes Test™ has a tendency to 'go viral,' uniting us in a familiar tongue. When I have taught the Shapes at speaking engagements, I find that they rapidly enter into the language of the families, communities, teams, and businesses in which I have shared them. This leads to fun phrases between friends and colleagues, such as: "That's so Triangle of you to say!" or "You're such a Circle!"

Applicable

The 600+ descriptions I will provide can be applied to any type of relationship. At a recent presentation I gave in a business setting, one woman asked the question, "Wow! Can I use this in dating?" The answer, of course, is *yes!* You can use them in any kind of relationship, from parenting to team building. In forthcoming books, I will explain how The Shapes Test™ can relate to specific relationships; this book, however, will enable you to broadly apply its principles to any of them.

Practical

This book is not an exercise in navel-gazing. The reason I chose shapes is that they have function. Shapes are used to *build* and *do*. This book hopes to be more than just an introspective guide. Physical shapes are better than letters or colors when it comes to provoking collaborative discussions, because they provide visual images. As the clinical psychologist, Jordan Peterson, says, "We feel through our ears but think through our eyes."[7] My aim is to assist you as you develop a friendship group, start a business, pioneer an idea, or go on an adventure with others.

My desire is that one day, every family, office, factory, and neighborhood would be aware of their Shape and use this common tool to do relationships better. I know that some people seek to purposely hurt, frustrate, or destroy others, but this book is not written for them. Instead, it is for those wanting to improve on how they build good things with those around them. Though I do not believe that this book will bring about world peace [and I'm sorry to disappoint its beauty queens], I am convinced that, for those of us who genuinely want to bring people closer together, it provides a tool to do just that.

It aims to tap into the good in each of us in order to bring out the best in all of us.

What?

For this to happen, you and I may need to improve our Relational Quotient, or 'RQ.'

A lot of emphasis is put on our 'IQ,' or Intelligence Quotient. Somewhat insightful, our IQ has a limited ability to indicate our potential success. Did you know that according to the acclaimed book, *Emotional Intelligence 2.0*, people with higher IQs only outperform those with lower IQs 20% of the time? Not only that, but more shockingly, in certain circumstances, those with lower IQs outperform those with higher IQs 70% of the time![8] People say that 'money makes the world go around,' but I disagree; I believe relationships make the world go around. If you have good character and can do relationships well, you will likely do well in life.

In this first book, I hope to answer three questions regarding your RQ:

Section 1: Understand Yourself

What are my Shape's strengths, weaknesses, and potential?

Section 2: Understand Others

How can I collaborate with other Shapes and resolve conflict?

Section 3: Make Yourself Understood

How can I express myself better and influence my world?

Each chapter contains new information about your Shape and some simple tips depending on the subject matter. I've also included quotes from some of those who participated in our various research groups.[9] Separately, we offer a companion journal that provides reflection pieces you can use to ponder what you learn. You can engage with the book and the reflection pieces on your own or with friends. I really hope it will help you as I know it has helped many others.

In essence, to shape your world, you will first need to understand your Shape.

So let's begin . . .

UNDERSTAND YOURSELF

1

What are my Shape's
strengths, weaknesses,
and potential?

2. 'Shtick'

What can I bring to our relationship?

Potential

Shapes

I'm a Triangle. My wife is a Square, my eldest son is a Star, and my youngest is a Circle.

What are *you*?

The Shapes Test™ asks seven simple questions. If you have not taken it yet, you will want to do that now. The aim is not to box you into one of four personalities. Everyone is multi-faceted, and you will likely find that parts of each Shape resonate with you in some way. In fact, the pioneer of psychological types, Carl Jung, said, "Every individual is an exception to the rule."[10] Rather, the objective here is to provide language that you can use or adapt in order to provoke conversation. With that in mind, you might want to encourage others in your life to complete it as well. It is free to take and can be found at TheShapesTest.com. Before you do, let me give you three tips:

1. Be honest. The test will only be as accurate as you are authentic.
2. Be open-minded. Don't try to force a result. No Shape is better than another.
3. Be quick. Don't overthink your answers or try to second-guess the questions.

Now that you have your results, let me give you an initial overview of your Shape. As I do, please take a look and see if the picture that forms in your head matches who you think you really are.

If you are a Square:

> You are likely someone who brings a sense of right and wrong, and you know how things should be. Your tendency to stay within the boundaries does not derive from a lack of imagination, but from an understanding that reliability produces the best foundation on which to build. In certain parts of the world, you may, at times, be referred to by others as 'a square' and seen as a stick in the mud.
>
> > "One of my life values is: 'Do what is right all the time even when it sucks.'" — Courtney | Australia | Square
>
> You question change, especially change that makes little sense. In your mind, change must be worth the effort because you not only want to do the right thing, you want to be seen as doing it correctly.
>
> Nickname: 'Goody Two Shoes'[11]

If you are a Circle:

> You know the importance of everyone getting on the same page, and you have a strong desire for peace and harmony. Circles often possess an emotional insight that can be used to help people understand each other better. You also realize that compromise is just an organic part of growth.
>
> > "I feel like I am the 'feeling translator' in our family. I translate our daughter to her dad and vice versa a lot." — Shannon | USA | Circle
>
> Others may sometimes find it hard to "get an angle on you" because they may not realize what is really going on inside of you. Essentially, you can read the emotions of others, but only

your inner circle may fully understand who you are. You are passionate, and when you feel a deep connection with those around you, you really commit.

Nickname: 'Rainbow Chaser'[12]

If you are a Star:

The world will never stay the same, and you know it. You don't mind it; in fact, it is often what switches you on. You are stimulated by competition; if not with others, then with yourself. As long as you have a chance to win, rather than threatening you, it inspires you. Your energy is a stimulus, and if you believe in something, you often find yourself persuading others of your convictions.

"We think we are the best Shape, that's why you put a star at the top of the Christmas tree!" — Jamie | Philippines | Star

Your sense of fun can light up a room. However, just like a luminous star, at times, your light comes in and goes out. Sometimes you are 'on', and sometimes you are waiting in the background regaining your energy. When you do regain it, you can give energy to others.

Nickname: 'Wheeler Dealer'[13]

If you are a Triangle:

You see things from different angles. You like to ponder why things are the way they are and get to the root of them. You believe in principles, patterns, and progress. You like to push boundaries, rarely settling for the status quo. Other people may feel you have an edge to you as you can be quite pointed or forthright in your opinions.

"We are the why-wonderers." — Shiza | India | Triangle

You prefer to share your ideas rather than show your emotions. You may be able to focus well in areas of technique or specialist skills, but lose focus when it comes to less significant tasks. Your desire for vision and your focus on the future often drive you to move things forward.

Nickname: 'Mad Professor'[14]

My hope is that much of what you just read was an easy, "Ah, yes, that's me alright!" However, I also expect that for most people, one or two elements may have taken you a little by surprise. There are three key reasons for this:

Firstly, you cannot squeeze every human being on the planet into four exact personalities. Our culture, experience, upbringing, worldview, and character supply just some of the infinite original-ity that each of us possesses. The Shapes Test™ is a stage, not a cage. It is not meant to imprison you but acts as a platform, pro-viding language from which you can express yourself to others.

Secondly, no one has a personality based on one Shape but, instead, a mixture of all four Shapes. The text you read will reflect your primary Shape, but elements of your lesser Shapes will also break through. [NB: You can discover the order and percentage of your other Shapes at TheShapesTest.com.]

Thirdly, and perhaps more significantly, The Shapes Test™ may highlight qualities you possess which you previously had not realized about yourself—especially when you apply them to areas of your life that you may not have considered. This is very com-mon. You are likely to be far more complex than you realize!

My desire is to both affirm the positive qualities that you already see in yourself, plus fan into flame the gifts that may lie dormant within you. This idea excites me because helping you understand and build out your Shape can create a great catalyst for the new and amazing possibilities you can bring to our world.

So what might those possibilities look like?

Average

I was born below average.

In pretty much every measurement, I am naturally below par. As an infant, I was so infamously ugly that when visiting the hospital on the day of my birth, my grandmother held me up to the window in order to double-check what she was seeing. To my parents' chagrin, without saying another word, she then returned me to the collapsible bed at the foot of my mother and took a few steps towards the cot adjacent to mine. Pointing to the baby she found there, my grand-mother declared . . .

"Oh, this one's nice!"

I always finished last at cross-country running, could never jump over the gymnastics horse, failed horribly in art classes, and had a slight speech impediment. I was expelled from my first school at six years old for biting the girls, and when taken by my parents to my local doc-tor, he proclaimed:

"Mr. and Mrs. Gibbs, Paul is a problem child and always will be."

And so, I have often wondered why I would be used to fulfill such an important vocation as the one I have . . . especially with the number of people I have met who have greater raw talent than I possess. Then one day, it suddenly occurred to me . . .

I was born below average to help average people do above average things.

The benefit of being born below average is that everything I do can be done by someone else. Anything I can do, any normal person can do. It just takes practice and a little training. When I see people, I see their potential because almost everyone I meet has more natural talent than me. That is why I'm an ideal candidate to empower others to achieve far greater things than I could. So, I'm excited by you! More specifically, I'm excited by what may lie dormant within you. In my mind, if I can help people harness what makes them original, then inspire, train, and equip them to use that gift for the greater good, I will be fulfilling my purpose. I guess that's my *shtick!*[15]

But more importantly . . . what's yours?

Understanding your Shape not only highlights the catalyst you can be for a better world, but it also will show you how you might help others notice, acknowledge, and encourage your gifts. So let's kick start that process by first asking a fundamental question . . .

"Why do you exist?"

Your answer will of course be shaped by your worldview. My answer goes like this: You exist because no one exactly like you ever existed before and God wanted someone exactly like you.[16] Now, I totally understand that this may not be your answer, but I am equally convinced you have noticed that there is something unique about you. For instance, I would bet my bottom dollar that you have a different set of gifts, talents, and qualities from anyone else you have ever met. Okay, so not everything about you is lovable—we are all flawed and sometimes need saving from ourselves—yet there is something special about you, isn't there?

But can you define what that is?

Potential

I once heard someone say:

"If you are thirty years old and people say you have potential, take it as an insult."

The inference is that by the age of thirty, we should all be living up to our potential. As much as I wish that were the case, I don't think it is. Most of us are not . . . especially in the area of relationships. This may be partly due to the fact that there are so few places we can go to learn how to improve them. In fact, most of the input we receive glorifies the *breakdown* of relationships. What is the percentage of movies, TV shows, or news programs that celebrate functional relationships compared to those that are built around dysfunctional ones? Exactly! Therefore, my role in writing this book is to help you first pinpoint the positive qualities you can bring to the world and then encourage you to build something good with those around you. So, as I share just one of each Shape's potential benefits, perhaps you can ponder if and where you already see it evident in your relationships.

If you are a Square:

You have the potential to bring *stability*.

It is hard to build anything positive without a Square in your corner! They can be the human stakes that root any plan of action into firm ground. Squares get the job done because they have a strong sense of responsibility to others. They are often the least 'showy' in a group of friends, happy to lift others up rather than being the center of attention. Quite often they are the unseen heroes of any team.

"I used to organize huge programs and do all the background work. I never wanted to be on show. I wanted to be in the backroom." — Praveen | India | Square

My wife, The Foxy Lynn, is a Square. She is utterly dependable. She always finishes what she starts, and her worst fear is an unchecked 'to do' list. We have been married for 33 years, and in that time, I have learned that I can count on her. We may not agree on everything, but everything we build, we build together. Everything she says she will do, she does.

If you are a Circle:

You have the potential to bring *harmony.*

Unity is a wonderful thing. It is also quite tricky! It takes a special kind of gift to help others see eye-to-eye and requires an ability to feel what others may be feeling. Many Circles place a high value on consensus, and their emotional intuition makes them sensitive to indicators that other Shapes might miss.

> "I want to bring everyone together and listen to people's stories. I want to hear everyone's side." — Mike | USA | Circle

Mike is a Circle and a good friend of mine. He helps me understand what other people might be feeling and, in doing so, he gives me the insight I might need to have a better relationship with them. I'm a thinker more than I am a feeler, and so I deeply appreciate Mike. Like a diving mask breaking the water's surface, Circles give me a view into an otherwise blurry world.

If you are a Star:

You have the potential to bring *adaptability.*

According to Bill Gates in his book, *The Speed of Thought*, success in our era depends on 'velocity,' the ability to respond quickly to people's changing needs. When it comes to relationships, Stars may be the best at this. Willing to take risks and be spontaneous, their zeal for solutions means they happily readjust what needs to be done and are ready to drop everything in order to help others solve a problem.

> "When the instructions changed, I shined." — Andy | USA | Star

Rob has been my friend since the day I immigrated to the USA. For much of that time, he was also a work colleague, and his ability to turn on a dime never ceased to amaze me. When things go wrong, Rob is rarely fazed. We all need people like that in our lives because they help us avoid getting stuck in our problems.

If you are a Triangle:

You have the potential to bring *originality*.

Often frustrated by the status quo, Triangles like to ponder how things might be improved. Triangles like questions. They like to ask them, and they like it when questions are asked of them. They are the experimenters who like to tinker. They need to know the why behind things and explore other possibilities. They bond strongly with those of matching beliefs, but also enjoy the space to see things differently.

> "Whoever is at the end of my thinking process will be served the best because I beat around the bush until I hit it." — Pat | Germany | Triangle

Wayne is a Triangle, and I have experienced the benefit of having a friend who is committed to a common cause. He has the ability to see the bigger picture and can point out the not-so-obvious. Lots of friends want to give me advice, but rarely has it been as well thought through and original as the advice I get from Wayne.

It hopefully goes without saying that *stability*, *harmony*, *adaptability*, and *originality* are not the exclusive gifts of their corresponding Shape. Neither is it true to say that any Shape is restricted to only having that one primary benefit. Although your Shape does not encapsulate all you have to give, understanding it can help you channel it.

Tips

Here are a few suggestions to help you recognize your potential:

1. Find it in community.

    As romantic as it may sound to go 'find yourself' on a mountain or an exotic location in the Far East, that's not where you will discover your true self. It is found amongst the people who know you best and those with whom you regularly interact. If you want to find out who you truly are, then you will have to face the good, the bad, and the ugly. All of these will surface over time in community. That is, if you commit to being with a group of friends, family, or colleagues consistently and take notice of what they reflect back to you regarding your strengths and weaknesses.

So why not ask those who know you best to fill in the test at TheShapesTest.com as if they were you, and then compare their inventory with yours. Maybe they will point out something that you yourself had not noticed. Plus, it may provide some helpful insights for my next tip on how to spot your potential.

2. Find it in a pattern.

    How do you spot potential? You look for a principle in a pattern.

    Anyone at any time can exhibit any personality trait. Although primarily a Triangle, I may sometimes be led by my emotions or want to avoid any kind of change and progress . . . but that's not my *modus operandi*. It's not who I am. As seductive as it might be to grab hold of an occasional reaction I might have or behavior I might demonstrate and want it to be who I am, it is better for me to notice the regular feedback I get from others or the consistent results I get from what I do.

    For instance, when interacting with others, I started to notice the consistency of people telling me, "I like how you put things . . . it's unusual," or "You look at things from a different perspective, and it helps me." Up until that point, I thought I was just pointing out the obvious to everyone. But once I understood that what I was saying was useful to others and attracted more support for what I do, I started to put more emphasis on teaching others and less on managing people.

This pattern of feedback helped me discover a principle, and a principle then inspired new practices that led to greater potential.

3. Find it in your frustrations.

If you have a latent gift, strength, or talent, something you have not as yet fully recognized, it may first reveal itself through your frustrations. You might get flustered by the inability of others to do what you think is fairly simple. You may find it exasperating and even express your annoyance when a friend or colleague cannot accomplish what you consider to be really easy. But take a step back, and take a deep breath, because that ability may not be as easy as you think it is. It is likely that your frustration is actually an indicator that it may just be natural to you.

Note: If it's your *shtick*, don't beat others up with it!

4. Find it beyond the first place you looked for it.

When I took a different personality test, the results suggested that I preferred to take something already established, rethink it, and improve upon it. But that's not really true. Instead, I love to pioneer things and start them from scratch. At first, I thought the advice to improve upon what is already established was incorrect. It was only when I applied it to *people* and not a program or project that I realized just how true it really was. I love to take someone with established gifts and help them reach their fullest potential—to be honest, I struggle when they don't.

You might therefore want to reread the description of your Shape and your suggested potential. Did you automatically apply it to one area of your life? If that did not make immediate sense, try applying it to another and perhaps it will come into focus more clearly.

Let me encourage you to start using whatever you found helpful in this chapter now. Begin to exercise your potential around those with whom you feel most comfortable. Don't settle for an introspective exercise in self-indulgence or excessive contemplation of oneself, but instead be inspired to positively impact those whose lives you touch. As you do so, you will also increase your ability to understand yourself better.

Your Shape can be your catalyst!

3. Spot Bowling

What will motivate me?

Strengths

Goals

Where do you hope The Shapes Test™ might lead you?

Besides using the personality inventory for many years on six continents, we surveyed various groups in businesses, non-profits, neighborhoods, and online. Taking people through approximately 600+ different personality traits, we refined our understanding of each Shape in order to make the inventory as helpful as possible. Apart from the standard interview questions, we also asked participants what questions they would find most helpful for a book to answer.

These three responses were the most typical:

> "How can I develop myself and help those who think, work, and even learn differently from me?" — Bethan | Northern Ireland | Square

> "In a career that values Stars and Circles, it can be discouraging. How can I understand my value as a Triangle?" — Corby | USA | Triangle

> "I'd love to know how to identify each Shape when people come under pressure and what is best to do in those situations." — Julia | Germany | Star

So what might your goal be?

Is it to simply get along with those around you? Do you hope to figure out how to resolve a current conflict? Are you working with a team and hope to win them over? Do you wish to stop people from misinterpreting your motives?

As a general rule, I rarely share my goals publicly. For reasons we will explore in a later chapter, declaring a goal has a terrible habit of derailing your ability to achieve it. However, a clear benefit to having a goal is that it can stop you from settling for less than you should. For instance, I may be at A and set myself the goal of reaching C. Now, I may only get to B, which is, of course, a lot better than A. However, without the goal of C, I may be happy to just settle there. Focusing on C, therefore, reminds me there is still more for me to experience.

Or, to put it a different way:

> Goals may not have the power to bring you success . .
> but they do reveal potential for growth!

And you have so much potential! Your potential is achieved when you capitalize upon the desires, values, and strengths that guide you. Each Shape has some specific virtues; focusing on them can act as a catalyst for your potential and healthy goal-setting. So, let me outline a selection of strengths that you may recognize in yourself.

If you are a Square:

> Where does your potential to bring *stability* come from?

> Perhaps it is your pursuit of *structure*, *organization*, and *correctness*.

> Squares rarely take shortcuts. When a Square reads this book, unlike others who might skip sections in order to go straight to the juicy indented bits, you will commit to reading it the way the book was meant to be read. You want to do it right and feel a sense of responsibility to do things the way they are supposed to

be done. For this reason, as a Square, you may reap the rewards of this book more than any other Shape. These qualities can positively impact your relationships. When fully activating your strengths, you will be a dependable friend who does what you say you will do and finishes what you say you will finish. Your sense of responsibility also leads you to keep confidence, meaning others can trust you with their secrets.

> "I like to be orderly and do things in a proper way and be faithful in my responsibilities." — Neander | India | Square

Being a Square does not necessarily make you competent at what you do, but your personality trait provides a determination to do whatever you are given to do, really well.

If you are a Circle:

What is it that helps you inspire *harmony*?

I would suggest it's your *intuition*, *empathy*, and *connectivity*.

You have an ability to make an emotional connection. A Circle who reads this book is most likely steered by the hope of building a deeper bond with a few, specific people. You are gifted with a kind of intuition that helps you see what other Shapes miss. People are likely drawn to you because of your genuine interest in how others are feeling and your ability to see the inherent good in them. Yet more than that, your higher-than-average ability to show people just how interested you are in them can turn this gift into a potential superpower.

> "People compliment me, saying, 'You bring people together!'"
> — Pete | England | Circle

Are Circles guaranteed to be compassionate? No. However, if you are compassionate, the traits of your Shape may help you care for people at a greater level.

If you are a Star:

What helps you bring *adaptability*?

Probably your tendency towards *flexibility*, *momentum*, and *risk-taking*.

To a Star, this book is a tool. Stars are most likely to cut to the chase in order to glean the information they desire. This stems from an ability to move quickly as you have a go-getter attitude to life. You probably have an attraction towards action and a good dollop of self-belief. You would rather do it than just talk about it. When this pragmatism is applied to relationships, you are not averse to taking a chance on people even when others may err on the side of caution. In times of crises, you don't like to get bogged down in negativity but move quickly to solve a problem. In better times, you can bring enthusiasm and spontaneity to any relationship.

> "To me, risks don't seem like risks because in my head it has already worked out!" — Drea | USA | Star

Stars love fun . . . but that does not necessarily mean Stars are funny. Yet, your desire for adventure can bring a sparkle to any relationship or team with which you involve yourself.

If you are a Triangle:

Where does your capacity for *originality* come from?

Likely from a preoccupation with *progress*, *strategy*, and *innovation*.

Triangles may be the ones who have the biggest issues with this book. This is because your desire to think deeply and improve upon things often involves a process of deconstruction. Due to your tendency to pursue high standards, you may push everyone else around you to achieve their fullest potential. The positive side of this is that you may do well at bringing out the best in them. Along with your preoccupation with ideas, you can help others take stock and find creative, strategically driven solutions for their hopes and fears. Although awkward and occasionally inappropriate, in the end, your persistent probing can bring numerous benefits.

> "Making a difference is my motivation for life." — Lathan | USA | Triangle

> Being a Triangle is no sign of intelligence, but your tendency to focus your brainpower can lead to breakthrough ideas that may not occur to others.

I am keen to point out that your Shape may give you a predisposition towards certain attributes and achievements, but it does not guarantee them. Importantly, the potential of your Shape has to be activated.

As the riddle goes:

> Three frogs were sitting on a lily pad, and two decided to jump off. How many were left?

> Three.

> Two only *decided* to jump off.

To take the required leap of faith and pursue your goals, you may need to understand the type of motivation that will help you actually get started. However, before we look at these specific motivators, let's discover the perspective that strengthens them.

Amoral

Personality is amoral.

It is neither good nor bad; it just is. Having a shy personality does not make you a bad person or a good person. Neither does the fact that you are either talkative or thoughtful, nor that you are emotionally or logically driven. You have a choice; your personality can be used to benefit others or destroy them. For instance, a great sense of humor can be used to comfort people and cheer someone up, or it may be used to undermine them. The deciding factor in all of this is your character.

Your character is the pivot on which your personality turns towards good or ill.

It is a mistake to believe that Squares are more competent, Circles more caring, Stars more humorous, and Triangles more intelligent than the rest of the Shapes. Talent, personality, and character are completely different qualities. For instance, your ability to sing has little to do with your personality or character. Yet, there is a connection, and they do impact each other. If your talent is *what* you can do, then your personality determines the *how*, but your character determines the *why*. If someone has a talent for public speaking, their personality will likely determine how they talk. A Star might try exhorting with enthusiasm, a Triangle might be more analytical, a Circle may seek to use stories, whereas a Square might concentrate on data and rules. Yet, in all of these situations, it is character that determines a person's motives for speaking in the first place.

This book is not about character. It is about personality. However, I would like to share a principle linked to a character trait that, if we embrace it, will strengthen our ability to build something good.

When I was in the Boy Scouts, I was very proud to receive two cloth badges. The first was for 'Arts and Crafts' because I made a papermâché crocodile. The second, and I have to admit my pride and joy, was my environmentally friendly 'Catering' badge. Did you know that as a young boy, I could go into a farmer's field, create an open fire pit, cook three sausages, and close the pit in such a way that the farmer would never know I had ever been there? Impressed? No? Neither were the girl guides . . . although it took me a little too long to realize it. At nine years old, those little patches sewn onto my olive green pullover were an opportunity to amaze others and win the girl . . .

Any girl really . . . I wasn't particularly fussy. Surely, my paper-mâché crocodile showed my artsy, sensitive side, and the undercover culinary skills declared that I was already a man about town!

Silly, of course. But then, have I really grown up?

As children, we think everything revolves around us. Yet as we mature, our thoughts tend towards others. Last year, our first grandbaby was born. She is a beautiful baby girl, and watching the effect of her upon my wife is enlightening. All babies cry with no thought of their impact on others, while a grandparent will go shopping and spend money on that baby with little thought as to what they could purchase for themselves. As we grow, our understanding of our strengths should follow that same pattern, turning our mindset from how our talents and skills benefit us to how they could benefit others. This eventually leads us to the following truth:

The gifts you were given are not those you possess.

The strengths you have are given for the benefit of those around you . . . and vice versa. Your talent for encouraging others was not given to motivate you; it was given to motivate *me*. Your friend's ability to sing beautifully is not a gift given to them, but to you. It is *your* soul that benefits. In the same way, as with your talents, your personality is a gift, but its purpose is your choice. Can I encourage you to grasp hold of this truth? *Let your love for others drive your goals.* This is the greatest motivator! In an ideal world, this perspective would enable all of us to reach our potential and bring the greatest good to those around us.

But is it enough?

Motivators

Growing in character traits such as humility, generosity, and selflessness will encourage us to make the world a better place. However, a little extra help doesn't hurt. We do not live in an ideal world, and I, for one, am not as selfless as I'd like to be. So, nurturing the specific motivators that help us reach our goals is also necessary.

If you are a Square:

> You will be motivated by *instructions, clarity,* and *responsibility.*

> You desire to be useful. You need things to be clear. You wish to know that what you are about to do is correct and aligned with the expectations of others. The kind of relationship that brings out the best in you is one of order and defined boundaries, where rules, tasks, and clear but generous deadlines are in place. You flourish when you can serve and feel secure that the support you provide others is appreciated.

>> "I like to make sure that, before I start a journey, everything has been put in place. Then I move fast. If I move slowly, it's because everything hasn't been checked beforehand." — Samuel | Ghana | Square

> At the end of it all, you want to hear: "You did the right thing!"

If you are a Circle:

> Your motivation likely comes via *authenticity, vulnerability,* and *affinity.*

> You desire to be acknowledged for who you are, not simply for what you do. You desire harmonious relationships with a few people whose story you know well. The kind of relationship that brings out the best in you is one where people's feelings take precedence and are made clear to you. A community where you can show and be shown affection creates an atmosphere in which your greatest traits can shine.

>> "I'm always trying to make my relationships stronger by clarifying who I am. By doing so, the relationship moves to a more honest level." — Sakhawat | Pakistan | Circle

> At the end of it all, you want to hear: "I need you for who you are!"

If you are a Star:

> You are motivated by *competition, variety,* and *excitement.*
>
> You need to be free. You want to bond with others around activity. You hope to have adventures together and move things forward quickly. The kind of relationship that brings out the best in you is one where you do things with others in a positive atmosphere with the possibility of a beneficial outcome. A flexible and exuberant environment where anything can happen is where you excel.
>
> > "There needs to be a constant challenge." — Reuben | USA | Star
>
> At the end of it all, you want to hear: "You helped get the job done . . . and it was fun!"

If you are a Triangle:

> Your motivation derives from *reason, independence,* and *significance.*
>
> You need to make a difference. You need to understand why. You are stimulated by the thoughts, ideas, and theories of others. The kind of relationship that brings out the best in you is one in which you are independent and able to influence those around you. An environment that allows you to concentrate on details, theories, and truth is where you thrive.
>
> > "In my brain, I am always processing the answer to the 'why' of all my relationships because when I don't find a purpose or value, then I'm not 100% all-in!" — Yarik | Mexico | Triangle
>
> At the end of it all, you want to hear: "You make a difference!"

One of the reasons I created The Shapes Test™ was because I saw many people use personality inventories to discover more about themselves. Once they did, it never seemed to lead anywhere apart from perhaps listing them on a résumé. Instead, can I again encourage you to set goals that impact those around you? Once you see the benefit your strengths have on them, you may be inspired to go even further!

Tips

Here are a few quick tips to aid you:

1. Set goals that are tangible.

   If someone were to ask you if you have achieved your goal, you want to be able to easily point to something that gives them a yes or a no. For instance, a less tangible goal, "To make new friends," is not as easy to quantify as, "To make three new friends." So, this second goal is better. Whether you make three new friends is not really the point. The more specific the goal, the more dynamic its influence upon you.

2. Set goals that are within your control.

   You cannot determine the reaction of others, so only set goals for which you can actually influence the outcome. For instance, if you are a Star, you will find that deciding "I will get one friend a week to take a risk" is less effective than "I will give an hour every week to encourage one friend to take a new risk." Ultimately, the success of the first depends on the decisions of your friend, whereas the success of the second is completely up to you. It is this second goal that is in your control and, therefore, more empowering.

   > "It was one thing to get yourself out of a stuck place, I realized. It was another thing entirely to try and get the place itself unstuck." — Michelle Obama, former First Lady

   In her book, *Becoming*, Michelle Obama realized that although our ultimate aim is to shape our world, starting with things in your control may be the easier place to start.

3. Set goals with the end in mind.

    You want to set both short-term and long-term goals. The benefit of short-term goals is that they are quicker to attain. However, where they really add value is that, once attained, they may provide the encouragement to go for more important long-term goals.

    Bowling Hall of Famer, William Knox, demonstrated the art of 'Spot Bowling' in 1933 by rolling a perfect game of 12 strikes— without ever seeing the pins! With a screen placed just above the foul line to block his view of the lane and the pins, Knox proved that you could do better by aiming at a mark closer to you that is in line with the pins rather than aiming directly at the pins themselves. He proved his point in a spectacular display. In the same way, setting short-term goals that are in line with your ultimate objective will be easier to hit and, just as importantly, will keep you on track.

4. Set out your stall.

    To 'set out your stall' is to communicate both your intentions and what you require from others. It is important that you let others know what best motivates you. Do not be afraid to ask them to provide you with the encouragement you need . . . *the way you need it*. Later on, I will suggest language you can use for this purpose based on your Shape.

Just to remind you, unless you are reading this as part of a book club, business, or small group, I suggest that you temporarily keep your goals to yourself until a later time. In the third section of the book, I will help you understand why that is important and how best to declare your goals when you do.

Next, let's ask: What might keep you from jumping off your lily pad?

4. Top Trumps

What could stop me?

Weaknesses

Pot

What obstacles stand in the way of you achieving your goals?

In the previous chapter, I said that your potential is more likely to become a reality when you capitalize on the desires, values, and strengths that drive you. However, as well as spurring you on, your Shape has elements that can hold you back. The more we ignore them, the further away we move from our objective to positively shape our world.

And that's a real shame! Every Shape is a potential building block in the Jenga of life. If you pull out, we miss out. If I pull out, you miss out. If too many of us withdraw ourselves, we all fall down. As much as that non-personal illustration may irk us, we must be strong for each other.

I'm reminded of a story I was told at a school assembly about three homeless men. After each one spent their days begging for food, they would meet together in the evening, huddle around a fire, and share the successes and failures of their day. On one particular night, all three arrived and were excited to tell of their little victories. One came with a carrot, the other a potato, and the third brought a meat bone. That evening they chose to do something new. Realizing that their individual items were not appetizing enough alone, they decided to throw their contributions into a pot of boiling water to make a stew. Yet, in the pitch-black darkness of a winter's night, as the pot passed around, the first man thought to himself: *"If I only pretend to throw my carrot into the stew and instead keep it to myself, who will really notice?"* And so, that is what he did. The second and third men had similar thoughts and, thinking that withholding their small contribution would not be noticed, they did the same. So when each of them dipped their spoons into the soup and put it to their lips . . . it only contained boiling water. Embarrassed, one by one, all three simply said, *"Tasty!"*, knowing that if they pointed out the guilt of their friends, then they would have to admit their own.

This is the only story I remember from any of my school assemblies. Maybe that is because it resonates with the sadness I feel when people keep their gifts to themselves. And we often hold something back, don't we? Sometimes, we even pick up our ball and leave the field.

Why might that be, and what might that look like?

Isolators

Our desire to withdraw may, at times, be overridden by our maturity and good character. In our surveys, people often talked about the ways they had begun to overcome their weaknesses. However, our personalities can still provide the Achilles' heel that affects our doubts, fears, and anxieties. When things are not going according to plan, each Shape may react differently, but the result can be the same: We are tempted to isolate our gifts and hold back. To be forewarned is to be forearmed. Therefore, knowing how my specific Shape is prone to this has helped me guard against it.

"For when I am weak, then I am strong." — Paul the Apostle[17]

Below, I have listed the primary way that each Shape may isolate both themselves and their gifts. As difficult as this might be to read, it may help you *acknowledge, battle,* and *confront* your behavior when you see the signs of your 'isolator' approaching.

If someone is a Square:

They may tend towards *self-paralysis.*

Squares orientate around service to others, but their desire to get it right can result in immobilization when things do not go according to plan. Paralysis can set in when perfection is not achieved, and they may begin to feel sorry for themselves.

> "I used to need all my ducks to be in a row, but now I find myself helping younger Squares understand the need to move forward when everything is not yet perfect." — Lynn | Square | England

A Square is perhaps the most likely of all the Shapes to see themselves as taken advantage of. As this takes root, they may begin to communicate as though whatever has happened only ever happens to them, and this, in turn, can lead to resistance and a struggle to move forward.

Synopsis: The Martyr Complex

If someone is a Circle:

They may tend towards *self-internalization.*

Circles are the dreamers and idealists who can inspire us. However, that can quickly turn to fantasizing and escapism when things do not fit their idealistic image of life and relationships. A Circle may then demonstrate a tendency to hide or find relief from unpleasant realities.

> "I chase the rainbow more so in hard times because that's the only way I get through them." — Mark | USA | Circle

In doing this, they internalize their thoughts and values so deeply that their expectations become unrealistic. On occasion, this may even lead them to withdraw by finding excuses or creating distractions.

Synopsis: The Escape Artist

If someone is a Star:

They may tend towards *self-preservation*.

Stars are pragmatic. They like to bargain and look for the win-win, but if things are not working well, the second win is the first to go. Although they like a challenge, Stars can become bored quickly and turn towards a path of least resistance. This may include moving on from others in order to reach their goals.

> "We may be the ones to gravitate towards the breakup anthems, like the Kelly Clarkson or the Meghan Trainor songs. 'It's their loss; I am better without them!'" — Jamie | Philippines | Star

This pursuit of what suits them best can result in changing direction on the spot and withdrawing their energy to reinvest it in a different place. In doing so, those who were journeying with them may feel left out and let down.

Synopsis: The Mercenary

If someone is a Triangle:

They may tend towards *self-reliance*.

Triangles are the agitators and pioneers who help us move forward. This stems from personal conviction about their ideals and beliefs. So, when others are not fulfilling their expectation of how things should be, their persuasions can cause them to go it alone.

"All the arguments I've had with my brothers and sisters are because I'm so positive I am right. Therefore, if a decision is becoming stressful to make with others, I'll simply make the decision myself." — Josh | France | Triangle

Refusing to comply, they may take the path that appears most significant and put people down or ignore them, withdrawing into themselves as they dogmatically pursue their vision.

Synopsis: The Hermit

For most of us, this can be hard to read. However, I am always pleasantly surprised by the self-awareness and acceptance of people as I list their 'isolators.' As gratifying as that may be, let me share two caveats to temper any discouragement you might feel.

1. There are times when our responses are justified. Occasionally, it will be true that your needs are being overlooked, and therefore you are right to highlight the injustice of it all. Sometimes people are being treated unkindly, and pointing to a more compassionate world is hugely important. It is also vital that, when apathy or atrophy sets in, someone *does* rock the boat and help us change direction to avoid calamity. And finally, there are many times when there really *is* only one way forward and your idea *is* the best.

2. Although these descriptions may be true of how you might isolate yourself, it does not mean you are destined to do this. Just as our strengths give us potential that is only realized if we act upon them, so our weaknesses present us with impulses that only hinder us if we give in to them.

So what can help us resist the urge to surrender to our 'isolator'?

Environment

Take responsibility for what influences you . . .

One day an old man was leaning over his fence. He lived on the outskirts of his village, and a visitor came walking past. "I'm thinking of moving to your village," the stranger declared. "Could you please tell me what the people are like here?" After some thought, the old man replied with his own question: "Well, can you tell me what the people are like in your old village?" The answer was immediate and delivered with an anguished tone: "Oh, they are an awful bunch! Mean spirited, backbiting, and critical . . . I can't wait to get away from them!" Without hesitation, the old man said with equal sadness, "Ah, I should probably warn you that in my village, you are going to find people very similar. I'm so sorry."

The young man thanked him and moved on.

An hour later, another young man came along and also inquired about the nature of the village. He again was met with the same question, "Can you tell me what the people are like in your old village?" The second stranger had a different story to share: "Oh, they are a wonderful bunch! Generous, kind, and encouraging . . . I'm so sad to have to leave them!" The old man smiled. "Ah, then I should probably tell you that if you come to my village, you are going to find people very similar. I'm so happy for you!"

The young man thanked him and moved in.

No matter where you go, you take you with you. Constantly moving in the hope that people will be different is not the answer. Therefore, to shape our world rather than withdraw from it, we have to proactively take responsibility for our environment rather than handing that responsibility over to others. To paraphrase the advice of a man who spent his early life destroying relationships but spent his later life building new ones:

> "Surround yourself with a great group of people who can encourage you in your strengths. Throw off everything that hinders you and the negativities that so easily entangle you. And run with perseverance the journey marked out for you."[18]

To help you do this, you need to recognize and address those negative influences that do indeed entangle and demotivate you. In the previous chapter, I outlined what brings out the best in each Shape.

Now, let's ponder what brings out the worst.

Demotivators

What discourages you?

If you were to build an environment that sucked the life, energy, and enthusiasm out of you, what would it look like? Also, what catchphrases might come out of your mouth when you are in danger of no longer pursuing the best outcome? Knowing these demotivators and noticing the catchphrases may help you guard against them and apprehend their effect on you. In a later chapter, I will help you start to reshape your environment by clearly communicating what you need from those around you. For now, here are some of the key frustrations for each Shape.

If you are a Square:

> You might be concerned by *waste*, *ambiguity*, and *disorganization*.

> Squares feel responsible. You are the guardians of the 'right thing' and whatever you do, you want to know how to do it correctly. If you are given ambiguous instructions, you will feel frustrated; if time is used wastefully, you will feel annoyed; and, if you are in the middle of chaos, you will feel more overwhelmed than other Shapes, unless you are given a chance to change things.

>> "I don't want to rush a decision because I might get it wrong. I need to see how it should be done first and be informed of the consequences of what I do before doing it." — Relie | Philippines | Square

> Feeling that you are being taken advantage of can lead you to believe that no one is paying attention to your needs or concerns

and that everyone else, and everything else, is taking priority over you. Your reaction may be to stubbornly slow down and disengage.

A warning sign might be your use of the words: "It's not fair!"

If you are a Circle:

Then you might shy away from *rejection, conflict,* and *superficiality.*

Authentic connection is important to you. You need people to be real with you, and you want to get past surface-level relationships. Getting involved in small talk may feel like a slow, painful death unless it leads to something deeper. Sarcasm will feel abrasive to your heightened sensitivities, and if you are in the middle of a conflict, then any hostility will upset you to a greater degree than others.

> "I don't want to challenge a friend even when I know I should. This is because I'm scared of seeing the look on their face if I upset them." — Christine | USA | Circle

The result might be that you take a step back from the world and hide your true self, genuinely engaging with only a few people that you feel matter to you.

Try to catch yourself when you feel like saying: "Go away, nasty world!"

If you are a Star:

You may be frustrated with *defeatism, inertia,* and *repetition.*

Happy to contribute, you like things to be upbeat. You desire freedom and feel that too much structure or responsibility works against your creativity. You don't mind accountability systems as long as they do not hinder success, and you look forward to any practical criticism that helps you improve. Inactivity will drive you stir crazy, and a lack of variety in your relationships may cause you to move on.

"It's not that we are uncaring, but if we are slowed down and if things are not working, then let's pivot." — Andy | USA | Star

When the desire to slip away from negativity and monotony is too strong, you may minimize an issue or use humor to shrug off the restraints that are put upon you.

Be careful if you begin to say things like: "I'll ask forgiveness, not permission!"

If you are a Triangle:

You may be irked by *ineptitude*, *drama*, and *mindlessness*.

You are led by your beliefs and convictions. Frustrated by inefficiencies, you feel great disappointment when something you value is done poorly. More than any other Shape, you might even question the point of moving forward if those around you cannot meet your expectations.

"Watching somebody do something without full attention and intention is like watching a train wreck—unbelievably frustrating and difficult to comprehend." — Carl | USA | Triangle

Your independence is important, and when called to execute someone else's plan, you need the space to do it your own way. If the expectation to keep everyone happy gets to be too much, any drama that ensues from you 'poking the bear' may cause you just to walk away.

Be mindful when your words imply: "My way or the highway!"

To manage our weaknesses, we must understand a paradox . . .

The irony of the elements that demotivate each Shape is that they can sometimes have the reverse effect. For instance, Squares hate chaos, but it can drive them to bring order. Although Triangles dislike ineptitude, it can force them to find a new and better way. Shallow relationships in a team may cause a Circle to campaign for time to be set aside in order to deepen them, and a Star who is bored may create opportunities for more fun. So what are the deciding factors between our demotivators causing us to withdraw or actively make a difference?

Firstly, the ability to influence the situation is key.

Without that opportunity, you cannot bring your strengths to bear and you might give up. So, where possible, take responsibility to change your environment. If you have little or no influence over the situation, then can I suggest you ask someone who does? Ask them to create an opportunity for you to shape your situation. If you explain how this will motivate you and how they may benefit from that, it might give you leverage in the matter.

Secondly, we must not vote in our self-interest.

Most successful people 'stand on the shoulders of giants' and, at some point, all of us are called to be the giant that someone else may stand upon. As a leader, I can often feel 'put upon' by those I serve or those with whom I partner. It's natural. It's life, and it leads me to ask a crucial question of myself:

What takes precedent . . .

My *rights* or my *responsibility*?

It has been said that as we mature, two things happen. Our responsibilities grow, and our rights diminish.[19] This is true. To mature, we must let go of certain rights and instead take up our responsibilities. In this way, the catchphrases of our past may be replaced by new ones. Let me encourage you to not only take responsibility for the elements of your environment you can control, but also take responsibility for your attitude rather than using the attitudes of others as an excuse to give up.

Hopefully, the following practices and principles will help.

Tips

Here are some tools I have found useful:

1. Play Top Trumps.

    One of my favorite playground games was repackaged, branded, and eventually called Top Trumps. When I was a young boy, I would buy some of these cards, take them to school, and compete with my friends to win their cards from them. The category of cards might be cars or planes or footballers, but whatever type of card it was, they all had a list of five statistics. Each round, one player would choose a category. If we were playing with fighter jet cards, that might be 'speed' or 'payload.' Either way, it would be the category in which the player felt that their particular card was strongest. The other person had to see if their card was better or worse in that category. If worse, they would hand their card over. If better, they would receive the other card, plus, importantly, it would become their turn to choose the category. This would carry on until one of the players won all the cards or backed down.

    The key to winning Top Trumps had nothing to do with who had the best hand of cards! Instead, it had everything to do with who got to choose the category by which the cards were compared. This is also true of life. To reach our potential, we must play to our strengths rather than concentrate on our weaknesses. That means putting your best foot forward and determining how to fight your battles or pursue your goals. Do not allow life to force you to play to your weaknesses; instead, take the initiative so you can play to your strengths.

    What cards do you hold, and how can you best put them into play?

2. Set tripwires.

    In the old Western movies, cowboys would sit around a campfire in the dark of night singing songs and telling stories, safe in the knowledge that they had set tripwires around the camp to warn them of any impending intruders. In the same way, setting an early warning system can be helpful when we are feeling demotivated. Noticing signs that your 'isolator' is approaching may give you time to rectify anything you can control around you. You could spend that time raising the levels that your motivators are 'in play' and nullifying any demotivators, thereby ensuring that your discouragement does not get out of hand.

What could be the early warning signs that you could put in place?

3. Plan a workaround.

When my boys were younger, we would drive to California from Texas for vacation each year—a two-day trip. We set markers along the way. We knew that if we could get to Abilene by breakfast and then El Paso by 6 PM, we were on track to arrive at our final destination at the right time. Planning the route meant that I would research it and ask the following questions: What obstacles might lie in the way of us getting there? What could trip us up? What might cause us to slow down?

Looking ahead for possible problems is counterproductive, of course, unless you do it to help you prepare a workaround. Planning an alternative route in advance that steers you away from the potential problem is a great way to make sure that, when you hear your catchphrases, they don't have to lead to failure.

4. Develop a support system.

You can sometimes cancel out a weakness with a strength. A member of our organization was asked to contact organizations, schools, and networks in order to create new opportunities. This was not her whole job, but it did make up an important part of it. As a people person, she did not enjoy sitting behind a desk. So, as a Star and drawn to competition, she decided to compete against herself. My friend awarded herself one point if she made a phone call, two points if she got a response, three points if it led to a meeting, and so on. Then she would add them up and compare her score to the previous month hoping to beat it. Because I was her boss, at the end of each period, she would religiously send me her score.

I never read them.

There was no point. Most of the time, I had no idea what the marks she gave herself even represented! However, she found that this made her stick to a task that she previously did not enjoy. Not only that, but my colleague had found a way to make it quite exhilarating. Notice, she came up with this idea, not me. Although I had helped her think through her personality traits, it was she who took responsibility for her own environment.

Can you also overrule a demotivator with a motivator?

As we close this section of the book, I hope you feel you have a good grip on the strengths and potential weaknesses of your Shape. We do not flourish best in *independence* but in *interdependence*. However, as we all know, relationships can lead to a whole world of problems, so in the next section, we will ask a crucial question:

How can we better understand others?

UNDERSTAND OTHERS

2 | How can I collaborate with other Shapes and resolve conflict?

5. 50 | 40 | 200

How might others see me?

Perspectives

Numbers

Let me remind you of the message of this book so far:

> *You are unique.*
>
> *You have potential.*
>
> *We are all flawed.*
>
> *We can do better together.*

This fourth point will drive the next section of the book because I don't believe we can do life alone . . . at least not successfully. It is true, of course, that we need each other. However, there's an issue because . . .

We are finding that authentic relationships are harder to build!

> "The average American trusts only 10 to 20 people. Moreover, that number may be shrinking: From 1985 to 2004, the average number of confidants that people reported having decreased from three to two. This is both sad and consequential, because people who have strong social relationships tend to live longer than those who don't."[20] — Ben Healy, *The Atlantic*

In a recent study from the University of Kansas, it was found that there are three key numbers when it comes to making friends: 50 | 40 | 200.

It takes:

> 50 hours of socializing to go from an acquaintance to a 'casual' friend

> 40 hours more to become a 'real' friend

> 200 hours to become a 'close' friend

It takes time. More than that, it takes work.

I am emphasizing the word 'build' in this book because real relationships need construction. They don't just happen. All relationships, the kind that last, require the type of intention that pushes us beyond certain barriers. Specifically, we must work through the 'veneer' stage, a concept I was taught many years ago. It alludes to how furniture is overlaid with a thin layer or varnish in order to protect it and make it look pretty. Only after a lot of use does the finish wear off to reveal the real wood. So it is when we make new acquaintances. Initially, we may only engage with their veneer, the side of a person that they want us to see, and the side of them that we would prefer to know. It may take those extra 40 hours to rub away the varnish and get to see the real them. This requires both trust and vulnerability on our part.

But do we give up too quickly because things appear to be going wrong . . . when, actually, they are going right?

You see, the friction and conflict that we dislike may actually be what draws us into a deeper, more authentic relationship. The very thing that can turn us away from a relationship is the very thing that has the power to make it real. In some ways, those extra 40 hours are similar to a signpost at a fork in the road. As we see signs of someone's true self, and as they see us for who we truly are, we each have to choose a path. With some people, we travel the path of withdrawal and keep them at a safe distance. With others, we persevere to create a meaningful relationship.

We cannot, of course, have the same level of relationship with everyone. However, have we given up too soon on relationships that could have been far more beneficial? Has our instinct to draw a tight circle around us limited the good we could bring to the lives of others . . .and the good they could bring to ours? If so, what might the pathway to a better relationship look like?

> "Each player has to understand the qualities and strengths of their teammates. In football, eight players, not eleven, win games, because everyone has off-days and it's almost impossible to make eleven players play to perfection simultaneously."[21] — Sir Alex Ferguson, Manchester United Manager 1986-2013

A 'better' relationship may mean different things to different people. For instance, to the legendary football manager, it might mean winning football games. To others, 'better' may imply a more intimate friendship, or for some, a more productive partnership. Whatever 'better' is for you, the journey to get there starts with understanding people's differing perspectives.

So let's dive in . . .

Cartoons

In a perfect world, everyone likes me.

No matter my personality type, in a soft-focused cartoon fantasy, I would be loved by all. For instance, in the Hundred Acre Wood, where A.A. Milne's imaginary characters live, every one of them is adored by children and adults the world over, and yet each one is quite different. Interestingly, many of the key players are perfect incarnations of the four personality types. In fact, now that you have been introduced to the Shapes, try to guess which is best embodied by Tigger, Rabbit, Owl, and Pooh and see if you relate to any particular one of them. To help you do this, here is my summary of their descriptions taken from Wikipedia.

What Shape is Tigger?

Tigger is Pooh's exuberant, happy, risk-taking friend. He loves to bounce, especially bouncing on others. He is full of energy, outgoing, and likes to have fun. Tigger is so overconfident that he thinks any task is "what Tiggers do best."

What Shape is Rabbit?

Rabbit likes to do things by the book. He always lets the printed word tell him what to do. He eventually admits that it is because he believes that he cannot think well enough for himself but proves himself wrong when he comes up with a brilliant original plan.

What Shape is Owl?

Owl loves to teach others and, although he presents himself as very knowledgeable, he does not spell well. Owl has a superior but kindly manner towards others. He likes to use long words that he may not understand himself, but he is motivated by a desire to help others find what they are looking for.

What Shape is Pooh?

Pooh is a friendly, thoughtful, and sometimes insightful character who is always willing to help his friends and try his best. He has a great love for honey and his pursuit of it, which often leads to trouble, forces him to neglect more pressing things around him. Pooh may, at times, be a little naive, but he is not stupid.

Let's see if you guessed it correctly . . .

Tigger is a Star.
Rabbit is a Square.
Owl is a Triangle.
Pooh is a Circle.

And, of course, all of them are wonderful!

But is that how life really is? If I took those same personality traits and gave them a human face, would it make a difference? Well, let's see. Let's remove the cartoon versions of each Shape and replace them with real people, each of whom could easily be described with a similar summary of their alter ego from the Hundred Acre Wood. I wonder if you will have a different reaction to their name than that of their two-dimensional counterpart.

Based on my understanding of each Shape, I would suggest that . . .

Queen Elizabeth the Second may be a Square.

> The Queen of England appears to be the epitome of that Shape. Just like Rabbit, she respects and promotes tradition. Her commitment to her responsibilities is second to none and has been proven over decades. Yet she is both loved and derided by those she rules over. To some, she represents all that is perceived to be good about the British . . . stiff-upper-lipped, dependable, and ready to 'keep calm and carry on.' But to some, she is the symbol of an unfair class system, a waste of tax-payers money, unfeeling, unimaginative, and stern.

President Obama may be a Circle.

> Charismatic, charming, and Winnie the Pooh-esque, he is loved by many and seen by his fans as a warm and affable person who wants to include and not exclude others. However, some view him as disingenuous, a man whose need to be liked has stopped him from tackling difficult issues. A man skilled in avoidance tactics who, rather than opening a can of worms, would prefer to kick it down the road for someone else to deal with.

Donald Trump may be a Star.

> No one is a better example of this Shape than the reality star-turned-President. Embodying the energy of Tigger, Trump is seen by his supporters as a man of action, decisive, and confident.

Others warn about what they perceive as his rash decision-making, rudeness, and impetuous nature. Some think of him as a menace and others as a messiah.

Steve Jobs may have been a Triangle.

The Owl of the modern technological world, the co-founder of Apple created a new path for others to follow. He was perceived as a genius who cared so much for others that he wanted to empower people with a passion to change the world by giving them the tools to do it. Yet many saw him as a controlling, dictatorial boss who treated those around him poorly and put his vision before the people who helped him achieve it.

So am I right?

Although these human examples are similar in personality to the lovable anthropomorphic characters of our childhood, is it not true to say that they provoke different feelings within us? I know they do for me. Now, of course, there are various reasons for this, such as their perceived character, roles, political leanings, and reputations. However, I would suggest that the most poignant is this . . . they are *real*. And you and I do not interact with cartoon characters, do we? No, we interact with real people, and real people are flawed.

The four examples I have listed would believe that they do what they do for the sake of others, and yet their actions are interpreted differently by different people.

Why is that?

Tunnel

Could it be tunnel vision?

The story goes that after World War 2, a general and his young lieutenant boarded an old compartment train—the kind you might see in an old British movie with a closed carriage containing two benches facing each other. The two soldiers sat opposite a rather aristocratic elderly lady and her granddaughter, a pretty debutante. The lieutenant and girl made eye contact and smiled at each other much to the disapproval of her grandmother. Suddenly the train entered a tunnel, and everything went pitch black. A few seconds in and two noises could be heard above the clatter of the train as it pounded through the enclosed space . . .

. . . a kiss . . . and a slap!

Seconds after these were heard, the locomotive roared out of the tunnel and into the light. Hearts were beating, surprised expressions abounded, and heads swiveled left and right as they tried to figure out exactly what had just happened.

The young woman was flattered that the handsome soldier had kissed her but was rather embarrassed that her grandmother had slapped him for doing so. The grandmother was annoyed that the young man was so brash as to have taken advantage of her grandchild but was proud that her ward had slapped him in return. The general did not know what to think as he rubbed his face. On one hand, he was secretly proud that his lieutenant had plucked up enough courage to kiss the girl, but he was also rather upset that the young girl had slapped *him* by mistake!

As the train carried on, the young soldier looked out the window with a faint smile, happy to have taken the opportunity to kiss a pretty girl . . . and slap his own general.

(I'll give you a moment to process).

I like that story because it contains the secret ingredient of all humor, a twist. In almost any funny story, laughter is derived when whatever happens is different than what you expect. However, not all misunderstandings end with a smile, do they? Therefore, it is helpful to get all the facts before we form our judgments, especially our judgments of others. As this story takes place in a tunnel, it reminds me of a well-known metaphor:

"Tunnel Vision" - the tendency to focus exclusively on a single or limited point of view

When we have tunnel vision, we can focus on a personality trait that catches our attention but may not have a broad enough perspective to see the full person. This, of course, is the methodology of 'gotcha journalism' whereby something someone says is taken out of context and blown up in order to discredit them. Gotcha journalism is purposeful tunnel vision, and most of us would never intentionally view others that way. However, the reality is that we rarely see people the way they see themselves. In particular, we miss their intentions . . . and that is problematic.

Why?

Because conflict is heightened when we misjudge a personality trait for a character trait!

So let's ask ourselves if it is possible that someone we saw do something bad could simply have been doing something different. For instance . . .

If you are a Square:

> You may perceive yourself as . . . *Responsible. Fair. Discerning. Observant. Perceptive. Not easily swayed. Trustworthy. Unwavering. Loyal. Supportive. Systematic. Sensible. Stable. Down to earth. Faithful. Person of their word. Traditionalist. Wanting to do the right thing.*
>
> You may say, "I'm here to help!"
>
> Others could perceive you as . . . *Sanctimonious. Moralistic. Bureaucratic. Jobsworth. Narrow-minded. Fuddy-duddy. Cardboard cutout. Lacking imagination. Holier-than-thou. Funsucker. Wet Blanket. Most likely to support a Police State.*
>
> Others might say, "You restrict me."

If you are a Circle:

> You may perceive yourself as . . . *Compassionate. Trusting. Focused on others. Pastoral. A people person. Charming. Selfless. Consoler of others. Nice. Kind. Deep. Passionate. Romantic. A believer. Wanting to include others.*
>
> You may say, "I'm here to listen!"
>
> Others may perceive you as . . . *Flaky. Scatterbrained. Too touchy-feely. Over-sensitive. Gullible. Naive. Deluded. Passive-aggressive. Sweet-talker. Puppy-eyed assassin. So heavenly-minded they are no earthly good. Blows hot and cold. Most likely to hug a tree.*
>
> Others might say, "You manipulate me."

If you are a Star:

> You may perceive yourself as . . . *Playful. Change-agent. Open-minded. Spontaneous. Laid-back. Daring. Mover and shaker. Pragmatic. Up for it! Bargain hunter. Sees all options. Wins people over. Negotiator. Copes with chaos. Wanting to get things done.*
>
> You may say, "I'm here to do!"
>
> Others may perceive you as . . . *Delinquent. Hyper. Likely to cut-and-paste. Fudges the issue. Skips instructions. Jumps the gun. Maverick. Cowboy. Loose cannon. Creates chaos. Short-fused. Cherry picks. Takes the easy way out. Only does the fun stuff. Most likely to press the big red button.*
>
> Others might say, "You use me."

If you are a Triangle:

> You may perceive yourself as . . . *Tactical. Principled. Progressive. Futuristic. Experimenter. Thought-leader. Logical. Fair-minded. Unique talent. Voice in the wilderness. Probably a genius.*

Objective. Completely impartial. Pioneer. Expects a high standard. Wanting to create a way forward.

You may say, "I'm here to explain!"

Others may perceive you as . . . *Know-it-all. Over-explaining. Armchair critic. Control-freak. Dismissive. Ruthless taskmaster. Rarely shows appreciation. Pig-headed. Cold-hearted. Frosty the Snowman. Lacking emotional intelligence. Madcap. Most likely to be on another planet.*

Others might say, "You belittle me."

So do you agree?

When you look at the list describing your Shape, would you say that the first paragraph is an accurate description of how you see yourself? Are you shocked by the second paragraph, or had you already sensed that was the case? How did it make you feel to read it? Have you ever experienced any of these reactions from your friends, foes, or family? Do they ever use some of these very words to describe you? Did they actually say these things to you, or do you just suspect people think these things about you?

Also, are you asking the question that most people seem to want to know . . .

"Which of these two perspectives is true of me?"

Who knows? Perhaps both.

One of the areas in which The Shape Test™ may distinguish itself from other personality inventories is that my end goal is to do more than provide a 'feel-good' book and, in doing so, limit it to a tool for self-analysis. Instead, it is to create a building manual for society. This requires that I provide not only the encouragement to get us motivated, but also the honesty that can turn it into reality. However, before we move on, let me share just a few thoughts to keep in mind.

Firstly, not everyone sees you according to the second paragraph. In fact, perhaps nobody does. There's no need to go on a witch hunt looking to track down any culprits. Remember, these are generic descriptions of four personality types, so please don't take this personality test too personally.

Secondly, not all of these negative perspectives are necessarily true of you. Then again, not all of the positive ones may be either. The reality is that many of these descriptions are, in fact, two sides of the same coin.

So, what's the point?

Well, it seems to me that the sign of maturity is the ability to put ourselves in the place of someone else, and the challenge of maturity is that, once we have done this, we need to be willing and able to shape the way we relate to them. People are free to interpret our behavior however they want to, and we, in turn, are free to interpret theirs. So let me ask a key question: Reflecting on how it made you feel when you read your Shape's second paragraph, would you want people to rethink their perspective toward you? If so, should we not also be motivated to rethink our perspective toward them?

Later on, we will look at how we can influence other people's interpretation of our words, actions, and story, but before we take the speck out of their eyes, let's have a go at removing any planks from ours. To do this, we must seek the ability to see the best, not the worst, in others. We can start this process by asking . . .

How do I broaden my perspective?

Tips

Can I suggest three don'ts and a do?

1. Don't project your motives onto them.

   We do this more often than we realize. We see someone do

something and immediately think they are doing it for the same reason that we would do it. This is always a problem and is especially so when we ourselves might have poor motives for doing what they did.

"Everything is pure for the pure of heart. But nothing is pure to those with a dirty mind."[22]

The reality is that we are not omniscient. We may be able to see *what* they are doing, but we cannot presume we know *why* they are doing it. Instead, where possible, it is best to ask a question, preferably one premised with a desire to see the best in them. Something like:

"Hey, I noticed you did/said this _____. I'm sure you had a good reason. Would you please tell me your reason for doing/ saying it?"

Now obviously, the tone of how you ask this makes the difference. If people feel there is sarcasm, a barb in your question, or you come across as patronizing, then it may create a bigger problem. So make sure that is not the case. In doing so, you may find, as I have, that this kind of transparency removes ambiguity, and a potential conflict can instead actually draw you closer to someone.

2. Don't believe the spin.

A common mistake is to base your reaction on another person's narrative. This is, in effect, placing the strength of your relationship with a person upon a third party. There are at least three problems with that. Firstly, a third party's motive for telling you may not be completely innocent. Secondly, their perspective of what actually happened may be inaccurate or incomplete. And thirdly, the tone in which they then pass it on to you could contain a different feeling from the intention behind what was originally said or done. It's a triple whammy!

Again, going to the source is best, so perhaps it would be good to ask a non-combative question premised with your concern, such as:

"Hey, I was told you did/said this _____. I'm just wondering if that is true or they misread what you meant. Would you mind telling me if you did so/say it and, if so, why?"

I have found this practice helps the situation the vast majority of the time. Often, I have uncovered a little spin in how it was passed onto me by the third party. A further benefit of doing this is that if you make going to the source a habit, third parties may figure that out and cease to pass things on to you with their added brand of mischievous interpretation.

3. Don't act before the fact.

    If there's one thing to learn from the train in the tunnel story, it is that we can jump to conclusions too quickly. As the saying goes, "Speak when you are angry and you will deliver the best speech you will ever regret." So, taking time to get the facts is a good thing. Sometimes the facts will negate the need for any action or reaction.

4. Do nurture a positive suspicion.

    The story is told of a monastery where all the monks were getting old. As they tended public gardens, people on picnics would see their work and chat with them, but none would join the monastery. This became a problem because, over time, the monks were getting older and their work would eventually cease. Because the monastery was in danger of closing, they decided to visit a wise hermit to ask for his advice. After telling him their predicament, the hermit replied that he had no answer for them. The monks were devastated to hear this as they had put all their hope in his wisdom and ability to hear God. As they were about to leave, he then told them that, as an aside, he believed one of them to be an apostle. Upon returning home, although disappointed, their conversation eventually turned to the subject of this mysterious man . . . Which one of them could it be?

The hermit had not given any clues, and so the monks began to suspect one another of being the apostle. All were therefore treated a little more reverently and with respect. All were now spoken of with high regard. All were trusted with greater responsibilities. The picnickers noticed the difference. What started as a positive suspicion turned into a new season for the spiritual community with young men joining because they saw a newfound love, respect, and honor permeating the group. The monastery was saved.

In his book, *Talking to Strangers*, Malcolm Gladwell warns us to be cautious due to our scientifically-proven poor analysis of strangers. Quoting Tim Levine's 'Truth Default Theory,' he argues that "Evolution . . . should have favored people with the ability to pick up the signs of subtle deception. But it hasn't."[23] However, he goes on to claim that this is a good thing! Why? Because those in society who succeed are those who enter it with a positive, not cynical, outlook on their fellow man.

My intention is to encourage us to persevere through the veneer stage of our relationships and not be dissuaded by our initial prejudices. Yes, we are all flawed. Yes, we are not perfect, not a single one of us. But I must not allow my prejudgment of someone's singular action to color all of their actions. I must not start to see everything they do as either good or bad. This will lead me down the path of polarization.

Later on, I will explain how a better understanding of other people's positive attributes can enhance our potential to build something good together. However, before we learn how to 'absorb' the good in other people . . .

What happens when we discover the bad?

6. 'X' 'Y' & 'Z'

What's the worst that can happen?

Conflict

Polarization

First, we might have to ask:

Is the bad we discover in others as bad as we think it is?

Yes, sometimes it is.

However, could it also be that, in a world where fear and division appear to be gaining the upper hand, we have followed society into a combative posture? Have we become more inclined to lash out than reach out? In a study that analyzed posts on Facebook over four years, it was discovered that users mainly shared information that confirmed their prejudices, giving little thought to facts and truth.

Elizabeth Kolbert, writing in the *The New Yorker*, reports an experiment in 1970 in which students were asked questions about controversial topics.[24] They were then separated into two groups based upon their individual answers. One group consisted of those with 'high prejudice' and the other with those of 'low prejudice.' They were then instructed to discuss the controversial issues within their separate groups. After this, each student was asked the same questions they were previously asked. "The surveys revealed a striking pattern," Kolbert noted. "Simply by talking to one another, the bigoted students had become more bigoted and the tolerant more tolerant."

Social media has now, of course, acted as a catalyst for this 'group polarization.'

> "This 'group polarization' is now taking place at hyper speed around the world. It is how radicalization happens and extremism spreads."[25] — Fareed Zakari, Journalist

Due to the algorithms used by many of the more popular platforms, the world you see is the world you want to see. As your posts and 'likes' show bias on an issue, your views will be reinforced by an internet that feeds you more of the same. In fact, after the 2016 Presidential election in the USA, a friend of mine said that she could not understand how Trump had won when "everyone" on Facebook was clearly against him. She decided to type into Facebook the hashtag #MAGA and was shocked to see her entire timeline change. Suddenly previously hidden posts from the other half of her friends filled her screen, and these friends were clearly avid fans of the elected president. I am sure the reverse of this phenomenon would have been equally true if she had been a Trump supporter prompted to search for #strongertogether.

Group polarization essentially works like this:

> The more you 'like' something, the more you will like something!

Now we find ourselves in a world full of extremes, pre-programmed to put others in a box and unsure of how to have a conversation with those of a different opinion. In this world, if I share that I believe 'X', then I will automatically be labeled as a 'Y' and 'Z.' This happened to me many years ago as I was introduced to a new colleague who immediately asked me, "What was the last book you read?" I noticed his posture towards me change the minute I gave him the answer. He clearly decided that because I had read that book, I was a fan of the author and all of his teaching. In actual fact, I was not; I just like to understand different people's perspectives. Moving forward, his behavior towards me made it equally clear that he had automatically labeled me 'one of *them.*'

Do you find that as frustrating as I do?

No one likes to be misunderstood or labeled unfairly. We all have shades of gray, and we all hope that others will see the good in us and the good intentions behind what we do. We want to be valued and we want our perspectives to be validated. We hope that what we can contribute will be seen as beneficial by everyone.

But what if it is not?

What if the things we highly value rub against what is highly valued by others? What if our perspective is at odds with the perspective of someone else? What happens when what we say or do causes so much friction that it creates a greater problem than we ever expected?

It has been said that:

> "A small rudder makes a huge ship turn wherever the pilot chooses to go, even though the winds are strong. In the same way, the tongue is a small thing that makes grand speeches. But a tiny spark can set a great forest on fire. And among all the parts of the body, the tongue is a flame of fire. It is a whole world of wickedness, corrupting your entire body. It can set your whole life on fire, for it is set on fire by hell itself."[26]

Have you ever wondered why something you said or did caused an unexpected firestorm?

I know I have.

Sparks

Conflict is more easily resolved when you understand what caused it in the first place.

The issue of saying or doing 'X' and then being seen as 'Y' and 'Z' is not the only thing in relationships that I find frustrating. Perhaps more troubling is this: what I may find aggravating, you might not. And vice versa.

Conflict hides in these differences, just waiting for them to collide. Pride, fear, confusion, and insecurity fan the flame, and things can get out of hand quicker than we expect. But, knowing what sets people off can help you remove the oxygen required for burning. So, what sparks conflict in the different Shapes?

Let me just give you some of the classics . . .

For a Square, it is primarily *injustice*.

> If you want to leave a Square feeling aggrieved, abuse the rights of others or marginalize them. At the root of this is an aversion to irresponsibility. They tend to care more about the person affected by the injustice than the person who caused it. So, when they see someone being flaky or negligent in their words, thoughts, or deeds, how that person's carelessness impacts everyone else is what winds a Square up so much.

> > "I believe people must be orderly and treat people in a proper way. I need them to be more faithful in their responsibility." — Neander | India | Square

> They believe everyone should consider how their actions affect others and that one person's recklessness or selfishness cannot be allowed to hurt the chances of the community, team, or family.

> For a Square: Everyone must do their duty.

For a Circle, it is often *insensitivity*.

> If you want to upset a Circle, you don't have to look far beyond their desire for unity. Harmony is key for them, and everyone should be treated with love and care. If a Circle believes that someone's feelings are being hurt by a system, they will not rest easy. If a person is being overlooked or not being heard, then you can be sure that they will want to do something about it.

"If someone is not being given a fair opportunity to contribute to the team, I notice how they may be feeling. Everyone should be given the capability of giving input!" — Clement | India | Circle

In a Circle's mind, we should all be tolerant of one another and accept each other's failings and flaws. Therefore, no one should be steamrolled by another person's plans, objectives, or opinions.

For a Circle: People come before programs.

For a Star, it is usually *interference*.

If you want to light the fuse of a Star, play 'the heavy.' Create rules, boundaries, and guidelines that hem them in. Then, constantly meddle with what they are doing. It will drive them crazy! Stars welcome structure as long as it provides them the space to give things a go and try them out. If their colleagues, friends, or family are risk aversive, there is going to be a battle of wills.

"The shorter the dog's leash, the more miserable the dog's life." — Reuben | USA | Star

What you might see as showing genuine interest can easily be interpreted by a Star as snooping around. A perceived overuse of caution and rigid accountability structures can label you a 'meddler' or 'stifler.'

For a Star: There must be room to maneuver.

For a Triangle, it is *incompetence*.

(Don't get me started!)

Triangles are big thinkers who like to think big thoughts and want to do big things. If something is not important, then what's the point of doing it? When something is being done badly, it's a big problem because whatever they are really invested in, they see as having significant repercussions.

"Apathy is worse than making no decision at all." — Lathan | USA | Triangle

If you don't view things the way a Triangle may see them, and if what they are focused on is not such an important issue to you, a Triangle may struggle with what they perceive as your passivity, neglect, or even thoughtlessness.

For a Triangle: It's all about the big picture.

Notice that some of these values appear to be in stark contrast to one another.

For instance, whereas a Circle might say that a person should always come before a program, a Triangle might argue that an individual should never come before the good of a system that will benefit far more people in the long run. In a similar way, if a Star wants to suddenly change course because they feel something is not working, a Square may say it is too soon to decide, a commitment is a commitment, and they should just pull up their socks and stick with it . . . at least for the time being.

Can you see where problems might occur?

I'm sure you can imagine many other hypothetical situations like this. Moreover, I expect you have experienced some as well. Again, conflicts rarely come down to one person being nice and the other being nasty. Yet sadly, conflict is exasperated when we misinterpret a different perspective for a different motive. This is a problem because, as the saying goes:

"When bull elephants fight, the grass always loses" — Kenyan Proverb

What's the worst that can happen? It is when conflict hinders a potentially healthy relationship and the benefit to our world that it might otherwise yield. However, avoiding conflict is not only impossible, it is unhelpful. Conflict is often required to get things done because it can lead to improvements. For the sake of building something good together, we must learn to deal with conflict in a way that does not hurt everything and everyone around us. But we still must deal with it. I don't buy into the idea that there are no absolutes. I do believe that some things are true and some are not. I know that differing perspectives can account for some conflict, but there are also times when at least one of us is in the wrong and should be corrected.

Yes, we have the right to believe anything we want . . .

. . . but not everything we want to believe is right.

You can have a real friendship if you understand that you cannot be someone's friend and their flatterer as well. Criticism and encouragement are both required because, without encouragement, relationships can be poisonous, but without criticism, relationships are so fluffy and flighty they do us no good. Real friendship takes a commitment to be compassionate. To be compassionate is to allow one's personal agenda to be shaped by the needs of others, and so, with that in mind, we may need to look at our Shape's natural *modus operandi* and bend it to help those we care about.

For instance:

Squares may find criticism oppressive but should try to temper their reaction to it.

Circles may steer away from confrontation but must be daring enough to embrace it.

Stars may offer blunt criticism but should be wise enough to soften the blows.

Triangles can be stingy with praise and must remember to give it more often.

Although learning how to avoid pushing people's buttons is helpful, it is not enough. We also need to be able to face up to conflict and deal with it well. However, in a world where "everyone gets a prize," are we dumbing down our abilities to the lowest common denominator due to the fear of giving or receiving offense?

"It's a catastrophe to sacrifice the good for the equal." — Jordan Peterson, Clinical Psychologist[27]

Some disagreements may never be totally resolved, but we can still be reconciled in such a way that we can not only carry on our journey together, but go on to greater achievements.

In order to do this, however, we have to tackle each other's gremlins.

Gremlins

Everyone has them.

We cannot pretend they do not exist. To get through the 'veneer stage' and build healthily with others, we have to face up to those elements that make us all hard to deal with. In his book, *Now Discover Your Strengths*, author Donald O. Clifton references the film, *Gremlins*, when he uses the following analogy to explain that our 'non-talents' can become monstrous when they hinder our purpose.

"But not unlike the gremlins in the film of the same name who were transformed into nasty little critters if they were splashed or if they were fed after midnight, irrelevant non-talents can mutate into real weaknesses . . ."[28]

Let me expound on that illustration. It seems to me that our weaknesses form a key part of what is lovable about us. Perhaps a friend is a little ditsy or forgetful, maybe a family member can get a tad sulky or moody. In the right quantities and at the right time, these vulnerabilities and foibles can actually draw us closer to one another. However, like gremlins who turn nasty when they are splashed with water, so our weaknesses can turn problematic when we seek to build with others. For instance, your friend's forgetfulness may make you laugh when you are simply socializing, but if you then start to work on a project together, it might create some tension between you. When relationships go beyond passive companionship to proactive collaboration, what once made someone lovable can now make them loathable.

Before we learn how to tackle each other's gremlins in a way that does not add fuel to the fire, let's try to understand how the different Shapes react to conflict and also recognize the typical reasons they might use to explain their response.

A Square's reaction can be: *Self-Righteous*

The Square may seek to judge.

They tend to be perfectionists and, having high expectations of themselves, they hate the feeling that they may have let people down. Squares possess a strong aversion to being told off because they are already their own worst critics. So, be aware that a light word of criticism can actually sound much louder in their ears than it is on your lips.

"If I go to make a change that I've researched and processed and planned, and someone questions me, I get really frustrated." — Courtney | Australia | Square

Squares can be quite hard on others because they are hard on themselves. They see things a little more black and white, right or wrong. They can appear quite stern in their response, especially towards people who ignore protocol, because they themselves have often worked hard to do the right thing. On occasion, Squares may deflect their sense of failure by blaming others.

Common explanation: "They need to be told!"

Circles might respond with: *Self-Protection*

The Circle may want to escape.

Keen to protect themselves and others from any emotional harm, Circles dislike conflict more than any other Shape. They will avoid it unless they see it leading to a deeper relationship, in which case they will pick and choose the appropriate times to confront people. Occasionally, they may develop a tendency to overreact and can be upset fairly easily when they are operating in an environment that they find abrasive.

> "I get called an idealist a lot. People are so divided, and I find myself translating each side to each other. I can see the truths of both sides but also withdraw when people don't live up to my expectations of how they should treat people." — Shannon | USA | Circle

Seeking to avoid what they might perceive as a soul-destroying collision, some Circles tend to use passive-aggressive methods to get their way. Externally they may appear to be agreeing with you, while internally they are already figuring out how to do it differently. Although they love openness and vulnerability, if they are in a heated conflict with someone, they are more likely than other Shapes to go cold and leave the room, at least until a later time when they hope an issue can be resolved more amicably.

Common explanation: "It's just not worth it!"

Stars can be: *Self-Assertive*

The Star may appear intimidating.

It's not that Stars like conflict; it's just that they don't mind confronting issues head-on. They prefer people to be straight with them, and they are happy to be straight with others. Stars don't enjoy getting bogged down by negativity. It's not that they find pleasure in putting people in their place, but they do need relational resolution before proceeding because momentum is important to them. With this in mind, they hope to assert their opinion and resolve the situation quickly.

> "I like when people are forward and don't sugarcoat things. I want people to address the issue." — Vilma | Albania | Star

As Stars express themselves in this way, they might appear rude and may even be accused of adopting bullying tactics. When on the defensive, their reaction might be to rant and rave in an aggressive manner in order to sweep the issue out of the way or, instead, minimize the situation, play it down, and use humor to poke fun and laugh it off. Either way, those they are in conflict with may find these tactics unnerving.

Common explanation: "People need to move on!"

A Triangle's response can be: *Self-Destruction*

The Triangle may seek to control.

For a Triangle, conflict presents an opportunity to understand others and be understood. However, because their typical reaction is to ask questions in order to understand the 'why,' this can come across as noncompliance. They like to have mastery over their emotions and control the narrative, which can lead them to become contentious when dealing with people or issues they cannot influence.

> "When someone tries to prove me wrong, I try to prove them wrong. I get offended if I explain my point and people don't get it." — Shiza | India | Triangle

They may be tempted to deflect the will of others by focusing on small details to distract from the main topic. Triangles can get caught up in denial of the fact that they cannot get their own way and may continue trying to convince others, even when their argument has become a lost cause. This difficulty in moving on can, in more extreme situations, lead them to destroy what they have built as they refuse to settle for any compromise.

Common explanation: "They clearly don't understand what I'm saying!"

So, what is the key to conflict resolution?

There are many books that explore all angles of that issue, but in this introductory book on Shapes, I just want to propose a suggestion: *Build a better environment in which your conflicts can be resolved before they even arise.* In this way, when things get tetchy, rather than getting caught up in the moment trying to figure out what to do, you will have principles and practices already in place in your relationships that will spring into action and take effect. In other words:

Stop *trying* and start *training*.

So, how do you build an environment that helps turn conflict towards good, not ill?

Tips

Here are some tips to create a culture for conflict resolution:

1. Build a bridge.

    You cannot drive a 10-ton truck over a 5-ton bridge. In the same way, you cannot bring a 10-ton challenge when you only have a 5-ton relationship.

    If you hope to move from a 'casual' relationship to a 'real' relationship, you have to build trust before you need it. If your relationship is going to last over time, then it needs to be strong enough to not only carry the normal day-to-day interactions you might have, but the 'heavier' disagreements, fallouts, and battles.

    So be proactive in building the following elements into your relationships, and start now!

2. Build a vulnerable environment.

   People will take criticism better and put up with your mistakes when they know that you realize you are not perfect . . . and you don't pretend to be. Be open about your mistakes. Although it would be foolish to exaggerate them, don't cover them up when you make them.

3. Build an appropriate environment.

   Only target actions and attitudes that people can change. It's pointless telling someone you don't like them because they are too tall. It is far more realistic for you to encourage them to become more patient. Classically, avoid exaggerating or say-ing, "You always/never." Partly, because it's rarely true. Mainly, because it infers a judgment upon them as a person rather than a specific action or moment.

4. Build a forgiving environment.

   Set a gracious tone and do not change it based on the response you get; this will allow others to gain trust in you. They may let off steam today, but at a later date, they will remember how you made them feel. And if that is good, then in the long-run, the rela-tionship will be able to move forward.

   "Be careful that victories do not carry the seeds of future defeats." — Ralph W. Sockman, Author, Pastor, and Radio Broadcaster

   Make sure you don't avoid that person after a disagreement. This helps people know that although you are judging their stance, words, or actions, you are not judging them as a person.

   Watch your facial expressions and body language. Sometimes your words can be saying the right thing, but your body can be telling an altogether different story. It's not a bad idea to have an argument with yourself in the mirror and notice what your face does . . . It might be quite a shock!

Praise in public. Challenge in private. The real key here is to control your emotions in order to give yourself time and space to deal with an issue gracefully. There's no point in helping people see your point of view and humiliating them at the same time.

5. Build a listening environment.

What we have to understand is that if someone is flustered, frustrated, angry, or sad, they need to get things off their chest. While they are doing so, there is little point interrupting them with your perspective because they are not listening. Instead, *while you are talking*, they are already thinking about the next thing they want to say to you! It is better just to repeat back to them what you think they are trying to communicate. Once they have drained themselves of their emotions, then and only then, will they finally turn to you and say, "Anyway, what do you think?" Now is your chance to say your piece.

In summary, we need to understand people's gremlins if we are to build something good together. That is best done by building a relational environment with a culture that turns conflict into collaboration. The great news is that, if you can shape the way you challenge others, you can be part of the process in which someone grows into their true potential. Also, we can all be the benefactor of this process if we are prepared to allow others to bring both encouragement and a challenge . . . which brings us to our next question:

How can each Shape bring out the best in me?

7. Shape-Shifting

What's the best that can happen?

Collaboration

Dimples

One of the questions I am frequently asked is:

"Can my Shape change?"

The answer is yes . . . kind of.

I have friends who have retaken The Shapes Test™ to find that their seven answers have altered and produced a different result. However, do we really change . . .or is it that, in certain relationships and situations, some elements of our personality rise to the surface while others are overshadowed?

This idea fascinates me because it highlights the possibilities we have to proactively adapt and develop ourselves. It also leads us to the further question:

"Do we change depending on the people we surround ourselves with?" — Elena | Germany | Star

Yes. Definitely!

We are dented.

None of us are the finished product. I have come to realize that there is more to me than I originally thought. However, left to my own devices and without the input of others, my potential to build something good with others has 'dimples.' I believe the same is true of you. The blows of life and a lack of opportunity can limit our view of ourselves and make us feel like failures in areas where, in actual fact, we may have the ability to do something special.

One of the skills I used to feel I had little or no ability in was public speaking. This was partly due to my nickname at school being "33 and a third," a reference to the way my voice sounded. My peers in high school said my speech was like a single-playing vinyl record being played at album speed.[29] I also have a slight issue that affects my ability to memorize scripts. And yet, today I travel around the world, accepting invitations to share my stories and present Masterclasses on various subjects because, although I have dents in my natural ability, it did not mean I had to give up. Instead, I made myself vulnerable to the example and input of those around me, and they helped me find what made me unique as a speaker. What I previously lacked in charisma, I learned to make up for in content, as those who saw my potential encouraged me to find my voice.

If I were to put this process into a diagram, it might start by looking like this.

This chapter concentrates on how others can bring out the best in us in order that we can collaborate together to build something good. Human beings are designed to be interdependent, not independent. Those we allow into our lives are key to drawing out the talents, gifts, and qualities that would otherwise lie dormant within us.

We must acknowledge that other people have what we need! It's not that we do not have any of what they have; it's that what might be hidden in us is more obvious in them. If we are willing to recognize that we have undiscovered gifts, plus acknowledge that another personality type can help us discover them, then we can move towards being the best version of ourselves.

> "Men are developed the same way gold is mined. When gold is mined, several tons of dirt must be moved to get an ounce of gold, but one doesn't go into the mine looking for dirt—one goes in looking for the gold."[30] — Andrew Carnegie, Industrialist and Philanthropist

This quote is often used when encouraging people to see the potential in others, but I want to use it in another way; I want it to encourage us to see the good in those wanting to bring out *our* potential. Sometimes we dismiss those who could help us because of an issue we have with their personality. Instead, in order to see the great qualities they can build out in us, we need to look beyond their flaws. This becomes easier when we realize that what we previously thought was a defect may just be a consequence of their different Shape. Once we have discovered this, we may be far more open to their input.

So, how might other Shapes help me realize my potential to build something good?

A Square wants to provide *organization*.

> Their understanding of order and right-doing can often bring a sense of mutual responsibility to any joint project. For a Square, any group work has to have a tangible purpose and logic to it, so they are often the ones to make sure that everyone knows what is expected of them. I like to move fast, but being married to a Square is a constant reminder to be considerate of others and give those who need it the time to keep up.

> > "I'm always in the stance of 'Have we told them? Have we educated them?'" — Sara | USA | Square

Another quality of Squares is that they do not have to be in the limelight. For me, that's a helpful quality that I can learn from. How can I serve with integrity when I may not be recognized for what I do? Some Squares I know have the ability to bring out in me a desire to serve the greater good without any strings attached.

A Circle will promote *empathy*.

That does not necessarily mean they are any more compassionate than anyone else. Yet they do have a great ability to sense what's going on inside people. Recently, my good friend Terry, a Circle, told me that she took the 'Eye Test' whereby you look at 36 photos that only show people's eyes and have to guess the emotions they are feeling. The average score is 26, but she correctly guessed 33. I scored only 21. The results do not surprise me!

"That's my hobby, to learn more about other people." — Terry | USA | Circle

Circles have helped me understand the importance of noticing how someone might feel when we are planning a project together. What Terry can sense through a feeling I cannot, but her example has helped me take more care and give more attention to how I express myself and argue my point. Along with other Circles, she helps bring out what sensitivity is within me, which I can then display in my own manner.

A Star can create *adventure*.

Stars have a playfulness about them that can help relieve tension and give us some perspective. When working together on a project with a deadline or planning a family event, things can get tetchy, especially if events do not go according to plan. Yet, many Stars have the ability to turn on a dime and find another way.

"I'm the last person to complain if I'm asked to change something." — Jamie | Philippines | Star

When things get tough, Stars are happy to bring a challenge to motivate others. This combination of playfulness and adaptability can bring out the dormant creativity and problem-solving skills within the rest of us. As a Triangle, who may try to convince others even when my argument has become a lost cause, Stars help me adapt to reality and let it go.

A Triangle wants to provoke *thought*.

Their desire to understand the 'why' is hugely beneficial. They can focus on a task, zeroing in on what can be done to improve it. This passion to deconstruct and then reconstruct can encourage us to rethink, refine, and sometimes redefine what we do. This is especially true when they also come alongside us to share their process for doing this.

"Once I improve things, I enjoy passing them on to others." — Hanani | India | Triangle

Triangles want a significant vision or goal for the end product and their desire to pioneer new ideas and systems may bring out a healthy discontent for the status quo within those they influence. Where we might otherwise settle for something quite average, a Triangle may be able to draw out bigger and better dreams from within us.

All in all, I am learning that Squares give me something stable to build upon, Circles cause me to become more rounded, Stars help me shine, and as a Triangle, I hope to help others see the point. Partnering with people in a way that awakens our hidden potential requires that we avoid the temptation to be offended when we are challenged. Doing so will ensure that our insecurities do not cause us to push positive opportunities away. Therefore, the real key to building out our potential is to decipher what parts of other people's examples we should absorb and which parts we should not. It poses the question . . .

How do I give myself away but still remain me?

Spheres

I would define your capacity to do good in three ways:

Evident potential - qualities that are clear to you and benefit others

Latent potential - qualities hidden from you that require others

Absent potential - qualities not given to you but given to others

When I say *absent* here, I mean this in the same way that a 'seedless' grape is seedless. There is no such thing as a truly seedless grape. Seedless grapes are manufactured in such a way that their seeds are inconsequential. They exist but in too small a measure to make a difference. Similarly, when my mother and father went to a parents' evening at my school and introduced themselves to my woodwork teacher, telling them that I was their son, he literally laughed out loud! He then informed them in a sympathetic tone: "Paul has no aptitude for this subject." He had tried his best to help me, and sure, I could bang a nail into a block of wood, but my talent for carpentry was so minute that, for health and safety reasons, it was better for me to concentrate on other skills.

How to use the knowledge of our *evident* and even *absent* potential will be dealt with in the next section of this book. In this chapter, the qualities we are interested in are the *latent* qualities yet to be awoken in us by others. Our friends' *evident* potential may act as a magnet to draw out our *latent* potential. I have seen this constantly in my own journey. Over the years, different people have come into my life and brought out qualities within me that I had not yet seen.

How?

First: They noticed my potential.

Second: They gave me opportunities to explore my potential.

Third: They criticized my efforts and then showed me how to improve.

So what was my role in that process?

1. I had to decide whether I believed they could grow me in that area.

   I'm not looking for one person to grow me in everything. I'm looking for someone with a track record in a particular area, not someone perfect in every area. Just because a friend is a great dad does not mean they will be a great public speaker. Although a colleague may be terribly disorganized, they might still be able to help me realize my latent creativity. In this case, one Shape does not fit all, and people's flaws in one area must not blind me to their ability to help me in another. Over the years, I've become less interested in what people say and more observant of what they do. Therefore, those whose help I accept usually have had some experience or success in the specific area in which they are 'building me out.'

2. I had to take a leap of faith and try it out.

   Context is key. Think about it. Sand on a beach is free, but put it in a plastic bag, sell it in a store, and now it has a price tag. Glue it to some card, and the value of the grains on that sand-paper increases. Refine it and use its silicon in computers, and it becomes a highly desired commodity. In the same way, to dis-cover your latent ability, you have to put yourself in a new con-text and step out of your comfort zone. When you do this, your skills, gifts, and qualities that previously seemed of little value will now shine in this new environment, because even the smallest of your strengths, used with purpose, can become far more valu-able than all of your strengths used without it.

3. I had to be open to criticism.

The sad truth is that our opinion of people is often influenced more by their personalities than by the fruit their lives yield. Those we dislike, we keep at a distance, while those we find easy to connect with, we allow in . . . even when they are clearly not qualified to help or advise us in our area of need. Some people are more forceful or gentler than others, and this presents us with a choice: Do I choose the most helpful, even if they are the most 'hurtful'? Can I encourage you to be bold enough to accept input from those who may not have the kind of personality you prefer?

I have previously said that there is no one we cannot learn from, and that is true. However, that does not mean that we can learn the same amount from everyone or that what we learn from every person is of equal value. It has been said that "bad company corrupts good character"[31] and so, if we want to grow our Relational Quotient, or RQ, we can benefit from an important principle taken from geometry:

"Relationships are *special* but relationships must also be *spatial*."[32] — Paul Scanlon, Personal Growth Coach

To illustrate, let me show you a second part of my diagram. I'm using Shapes here simply as an example, but you can replace these spheres with the name of individuals or people groups.

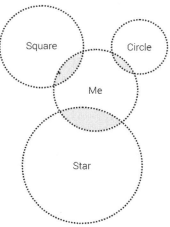

95

It is foolish to declare, "I am not easily influenced." Yes, you are! We all are! Trying not to be easily influenced is a wasteful pursuit. A wise person will accept that fact and instead focus on these two questions:

Who is it that I want to influence me most?

What should I absorb from them and what should I not?

Your RQ is linked to your ability to create the right volume in your various relationships. Do you give too much space in your life to those who are a negative influence upon you? I am not suggesting that you completely get rid of them—you may still be a mutual benefit to each other; however, you may want to give them less space . . . less time . . . less opportunity for their negativity or ambivalent attitude to influence you. Are you giving enough space to those who are a positive influence upon you? You may want to give them an invitation and permission to bring that influence to an even greater degree. When you do, here's what to remember:

You want to learn *from* them but not *become* them!

There are many great people in this world that I admire, but I'm happy in my own skin. I hope you are as well. I have met people who wish they were someone else. I have even known people admit to lying when completing The Shapes Test™ because they felt that being one Shape would be better than another. I believe this is because they have yet to realize who they can be and the good they can bring to the world. Sadly, some of us have yet to discover all the gold that lies within us. I'm really hoping that The Shapes Test™ will change that and together we can collaborate to build something great. For this to happen, we need to understand what elements of another person can draw out our potential and which parts we can only admire from a distance.

This is illustrated in the third part of my diagram.

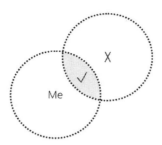

My heroes are magnetic to me, but I must not become a mirror image of them! If we idealize people too much and compare ourselves to them, we will damage our own sense of identity and neglect the unique qualities that we were born with. Therefore, I have tried to figure out what I can copy from those I admire and what I cannot. Terry is empathetic, and Jamie is highly adaptable. They build out my latent potential in those important areas. They also help me realize something else: *I'm not Terry, and I am not Jamie.* I can't be and don't want to be. I want to be me.

But who is 'me'?

Later we will explore how you can answer that question, but first let's focus on how we can recognize the benefits of our Shape without being limited by it. Your Shape should be your servant; you should not become its slave!

Change

Collaboration involves relational compromise in its best sense.

Specifically in this chapter, we are looking at how collaboration requires you to be changed by the positive influence of others as they 'get the best out of you.' Therefore, once you know whose influence you wish to increase and decrease in your life, you have to face a more challenging question: What's stopping you from changing?

Certain Shapes need certain things to be in place to help them develop. Again, the following information is meant to give you understanding and the ability to take control. I am not saying that unless you have these things in place, you cannot grow; I am saying that if you want to grow, then where possible, adding these elements into your life may be helpful.

As a Square, you need *time*.

Specifically, time to process.

You want to know the steps that are required, and you want to make sure that the reason for those steps makes sense. You don't want to be rushed into decisions because you might get it wrong. Ideally, you want to attempt any change with as little risk as possible. Small reversible steps are more attractive to you.

"If I feel rushed into decisions, I can freeze up depending on how overwhelmed I am that day." — Christine | USA | Square

So, don't feel you have to rush growth. Discovering and developing yourself with the help of others is not a competition. Don't beat yourself up because it's taking a while. Don't go on a guilt trip, feel sorry for yourself, and give up. Relax and enjoy the journey. Perhaps you might want to use your love for structure to map out a plan with those who are helping you, and then follow it step by step.

As a Circle, you want to feel it's *the right thing to do*.

To feel right, it must have the best interest of others at heart.

You find it harder to be happy with any transition you make in your behavior if those impacted by it are not comfortable. The whole room doesn't have to be perfectly in sync, but if you're going to attempt any adjustments, it is important that those who may be impacted are given a place to express their feelings.

"I want to journey with people and have conversations to help them be okay with change." — Pete | England | Circle

Broken promises will affect you negatively, so spend extra time communicating your expectations to those you want to help you. In this way, you can do your best to ensure they know how to follow through with any support they are offering.

As a Star, you hope it creates *momentum*.

Ideally, it will remove an obstacle in your way.

You will want any change you undertake to be forward-looking, positive, and realistic. Tangible results will spur you on. You will be highly motivated to change if you can clearly see a problem that will be solved or an achievement that can be attained. You will also find any change more exciting if it means that you can compete against your old self and become a better you.

"My number one advocate is me—I'm always competing against myself." — Isaac | USA | Star

When planning on change, especially personal change, it may be good for you to ask your collaborators to set challenges for you to reach. Completing these stages gives you the opportunity to relax, have fun, and celebrate each achievement. You will likely be spurred on by anything that gives you a sense of fighting for a good cause with moments of victory along the way.

As a Triangle, you crave *ownership*.

You want to create change rather than simply execute it.

You need the option to analyze and debate any reconstruction—ideally with others, but at the very least, within your own head. The problem with any change may be that you keep wanting to improve upon it. Therefore, change itself may not be the problem;

for you, the issue may be knowing when to accept a change that everyone else is happy with, and then move on.

> "Sometimes it's hard for me to admit that my way may not be the best way. It is difficult for me in a working environment if I'm not given the reason why, but I'm still expected to follow the instructions I am given." — Yarik | Mexico | Triangle

When a change is presented, you will want to know the reason it is necessary. As Triangles, however, our motive should be to ask the 'why' in order to understand rather than looking for an excuse to avoid it. Asking your role models for a chance to paint the big picture together is always going to prove beneficial to both of you. It gives you the chance to shape the journey and gives them the opportunity to inspire you.

Change is inevitable. Change is healthy. Change is good!

Our bodies are constantly changing. In fact, biologically, you are not the same person you were! Almost every cell in your body is constantly being replaced.[33] We cannot choose *if* we change, only *how* we change. Therefore, keeping an open mind is commonly understood to be a good thing.

> "Intelligent people are always open to ideas. In fact, they look for them."[34] — King Solomon

So, can I encourage you to search out those who see greater potential in you? Change will always involve growing pains, but it is worth it. Your Shape is meant to help you understand yourself better, but if you allow yourself to be restricted by it in any way, that would be a tragedy.

You want definition without limitation!

Tips

Here are some generic boxes to avoid putting yourself in.

1. The 'Time' Box.

    A while back I bumped into an old friend and told them I was a Triangle. They laughed: "No, you're not! Surely you're a Star!" I totally understood their reaction because in the role they had previously seen me in, I had little responsibility. In those situations, my playfulness and ability to cause mischief definitely trumped my need to focus and make progress, qualities I now need leading an international organization. They had frozen me in time.

    Many labels are sticky. You can peel off the label, but the glue that stuck it down for such a long time may prove harder to remove. In the same way, *you* can change, but the gooey gunge of your reputation may take another couple of years to be slowly scratched away. During that time, keep persevering. Don't get defensive when people keep reminding you of your previous flaws or limitations. Accept that is who you were and admit it to others, but then invite them to encourage you as they see you change and pursue your goals.

2. The 'Identity' Box.

    Shapes, like water, can take the shape of the container they are put in; therefore, the environment you find yourself in may affect which parts of your personality become most evident. As I said earlier, if you are in a group with a lot of disorganization, you might find that, if your secondary Shape is a Square, it rises to the top as a reaction to the need that presents itself. Rather than running away because you desire order, I suggest you ask others if they can help you use that desire to bring the structure you can see is missing. In one of our survey interviews, a member of a software company highlighted this by saying:

"I actually love disorganization and chaos. It energizes me, and I love bringing organization to the situation—it may cause me stress, but I view that stress as adrenaline." — Stephanie | USA | Square

Your secondary Shape[35] may become more prominent than your primary Shape for the period of time you are in that new 'container.' However, over a prolonged period of time, you might see yourself Shape-shift more permanently because that is the best way you can bring good to your world. So, don't allow your Shape to become your identity, because the size of your character is far more important than the shape of your personality.

3. The 'Behavior' Box.

    I have to be careful not to limit myself by making excuses. Our Shape can be a get-out-of-jail-free card for any behaviors or weaknesses we want to avoid addressing. "I'm a Triangle, so that's why I use harsh language!" Maybe . . . or perhaps that's just because I'm obnoxious!

    Your Shape is a tool. It presents an opportunity to influence the outcome of your relationships as long as you do not fall into the temptation of becoming a prisoner or victim to your personality type.

So, now that we have gained a little insight into how to collaborate with others to help us discover our *latent* potential, what about our *evident* and *absent* potential? How do we collaborate with others to build something good together and ask for help without giving the impression we are needy? How do we communicate that we have something good to offer without people thinking we've gotten too big for our boots?

To put it simply, how do we make ourselves better understood?

MAKE YOURSELF UNDERSTOOD

3 How can I express myself better and influence my world?

8. Citizenship

Who do I say I am?

Definition

Awareness

When you say "me" . . . what do you mean?

And exactly what are you trying to communicate?

In 2005, my wife, our two boys, and I left England for the USA, packing all we owned in the world into seven suitcases. At the first restaurant we visited in the States, the waitress, who was clearly confused by my Mancunian accent, asked me to repeat my order three times. The fourth time she asked me in Spanish!

It is said that the UK and USA are separated by a common language, and this has led to humorous incidents over the years. However, the inability to be understood can be frustrating, especially when we are interacting with those we feel should know us better. Yet, even with our friends, our words travel through various filters before they are heard. The background, culture, life experiences, and vernacular, of both the speaker and hearer, provide just some of the opportunities for confusion. In his book, *Talking to Strangers*,[36] Malcolm Gladwell makes this point by describing the meeting of two very different people, Cortés and Montezuma, who met for the first time in 1519AD and whose misunderstanding ultimately led to the deaths of an estimated 10 million people.

In a communication obstacle course, our words need to be as clear as a Marine is tough.

If you want to build something good with others, the ability to succinctly define who you are is hugely beneficial. Many years ago, a budget airline gave me a valuable lesson regarding its two main advantages. In my thirties, I had begun to make more transatlantic flights due to increased speaking engagements, and this made me more aware of the differences between airlines. If I had a choice, I would choose the ones that provided my favorite English delights free of charge: chunky Kit Kats, Cornish pasties, and English breakfasts. A free toothbrush and woolly socks could also turn my eye!

However, one Saturday night as I was traveling from Manchester to Belfast with a cheap and cheerful airline, I flew out accompanied by an army of Northern Irish Manchester United fans who were returning home from a big match. The atmosphere in the airport was chaotic. At one point, a group tried to start a fight with me. However, the most extraordinary thing on that trip was the 'welcome' by the flight attendant who tried to communicate amidst a roar of football chants, expletives, and general pandemonium. I cannot recall her precise words, but they went something like this:

> "Listen, you lot! We've already contacted the Belfast police. If you give me any trouble, I'll have you locked away! Don't touch me. Don't even speak to me . . ."

After giving the standard safety talk, she concluded her motivational speech with:

> ". . . *Now shut up and belt up!*"

I just sat there. I would have liked to have gone to the bathroom, but I wasn't willing to take the risk. Then I noticed something strange; I was in no way disappointed. There was no entertainment system or travel packs, and I had to pay for my chunky Kit Kat. But I was completely content.

Why?

Because this particular airline had clearly defined itself. It promised only two things—to be cheap, which it was, and to get me there on time, which it did. The airline's brand was clear and simple: We aim to be the cheapest and most reliable, but don't expect frills.

There are two important benefits to being able to clearly define yourself:

1. It warns people of what they should not expect of you.

2. It holds you accountable for what they should expect of you.

Both are extremely helpful.

I don't have to be everything as long as I bring something, and when people know what I cannot give—my absent potential—it then frees me to concentrate on my strengths rather than my weaknesses. Also, when I do bring whatever I have to offer—my evident and latent potential—they hold me accountable, challenging me to take even greater steps of faith with my gifts, talents, and personality traits. I welcome such encouragement and like to surround myself with people who will spur me on to give my best.

To reap the benefits of definition, I have to accurately describe myself and, to do that, I cannot play guessing games because definition is useless if people see a disconnect between who I think I am and who I really am.

So, how self-aware are you?

Passport

It seems to me that there are two basic pathways to self-discovery:

1. What you see yourself do.

2. What people say about you.

The first path is helpful if you pay attention to the fruit of your actions.

We all have something to 'bring to the party,' and actually, how you behave at a social event can highlight your attributes. This may be due to fewer outside forces influencing our behavior, such as company rules, club policies, or formal etiquette. Generally speaking, a party provides a blank sheet that frees you to be who you truly are. Not only that, but it can highlight the wider qualities you offer society. So, what gifts do you bring to such an event? At first glance, we might think everyone goes to a relaxing get-together for the same reason . . . to have fun, right? However, having fun may mean something different to a Star than it does to a Circle. So let's look at what happens when the four Shapes attend a shindig.

When a Square goes to a party:

> You may spend much of your time checking that everyone has what they need and that no one or nothing is being left out. This is especially true when you are organizing a party; however, subconsciously as a guest, you may still have a checklist without realizing it. If you have a close relationship with your host, you may find yourself offering them your assistance.

>> "If I try to organize people, it's just the way I am. Even at a party, I have to stop myself giving advice to the party planner." — Becca | England | Square

> Here are questions I've known Squares to ask before, during, and after a social function: *Was everyone given the correct time and location? Does anyone need a ride? Is everyone enjoying themselves? Can I talk to you in a moment—I just need to make sure everyone has _____? Can you call me when you get home so I know you got back okay?*

In life, do you find yourself making sure that everything that needs to be in place is taken care of? Do you focus on finding or creating structures for success? If you do, it proves my point that it is hard to build anything without a Square in your corner . . . even a good party!

When a Circle goes to a party:

You are looking to connect. Although at times you may be a social butterfly, it's likely that your preference is to leave the party having a deeper relationship with one or two people.

"I like close friendships, I like one on one, I like quality time."
— Keren | England | Circle

When a Circle enters the room, some of the things on their mind are: *Who is here that I know really well? Is there a new potential friend I can win over? Who can I spend the evening with? I wonder how _____ is feeling about _____? Is there someone whose pain I can soothe, or can they soothe mine? Who can I share my dreams with, and who has a dream I can encourage them in?*

Have you noticed that you help people stick together when things might otherwise pull them apart? Do you find ways for people to get on the same page? I bet you do, because it is Circles who often bring the relational glue to a group of people!

When a Star goes to the party:

You might want to let off some steam and, if so, everyone is going to know you are there. Fun is what you are looking for, and if you are aware that you may not be the wittiest person in the room, you will make up for it with props such as a humorous T-shirt, gimmicks, or encouraging some kind of fun activity. You probably don't mind making a fool of yourself if you can leave the room knowing you made it memorable.

"I'll be one to wear strong colored clothes and a big hat!" — Melissa | Brasil | Star

A Star's proactive nature is often reflected at a party through the following thoughts: *How do I get this party started?! Who can I make laugh? What might be a fun activity to get people involved in? This is boring—how can I light a fire under these people? How on earth can I have fun unless everyone else is? Who can I get to join me to help me create a bit of fun?*

Have you occasionally found yourself to be the center of attention? Do you stir up other people? Do you inject a bit of life into a party or situation when you know it needs it? It would not surprise me if you do, because Stars can bring smiles to our faces, lighten the load of our hearts, and help us get over the bumps in the road!

If a Triangle goes to the party:

Someone made you go. You can probably think of a number of more important things you could be doing with your time. However, there are many reasons a Triangle can enjoy the party, most of which extend beyond the party itself.

Here are some of the questions you might be pondering when you find yourself at such an event: *Why on earth am I here? What productive thing could come out of me being here? Is there someone I can connect with for a purpose bigger than this party? Who can I have a discussion with about this idea on my mind?*

"My friends don't like me at parties because I ask these questions every time." — Jaine | Brasil | Triangle

You may not be a party animal, but do you notice that, in life as well as at parties, you can often turn meaningless conversations into constructive discussions? Do you find yourself looking for meaning and being more intentional than those around you? Of course you do! It's Triangles who help us find purpose!

Rather than box you into a personality type, I'm hoping these descriptions give you a platform from which to both differentiate yourself from others and express yourself. If we want people to pivot their expectations of us towards our strengths, not our weaknesses, our *evident* and *latent* potential, not our *absent* potential, then we must make sure that when we describe ourselves, we do so in line with our true qualities.

This is our passport to definition.

When we first arrived in the States in 2005, we intended to stay for around two years, but we fell in love with the US, the people we met, and the opportunity it provided to grow our organization. So, after a very lengthy, complicated, and frustrating process, we became US citizens in 2016.

During the citizenship ceremony, I was asked a question that completely took me by surprise . . .

"What would you like your name to be?"

I was told that, as a new citizen, I was being offered a new start and was being given the opportunity to legally rename myself. In essence, I could decide how I would be known to others from that day forward. I was momentarily stunned. I never knew this was going to be an option. Afterwards, I wondered, if I had been given more time to think about it, would I have renamed myself? I doubt it. However, it did raise an interesting question in my mind:

In reality, how easy is it to define who you are to others?

It isn't.

The offer to change my name was something I was entitled to, but it was not a magic wand. I can ask people to think of me a certain way, but they are going to think of me in whatever way they wish to. If I want a certain reputation, I need to earn it; I am not entitled to it. I must not get frustrated or angry with others, but instead, calmly take responsibility to give them the information that they need to see me in a new light and then model who I say I am. If we misrepresent ourselves, people may second-guess our intentions. However, if our behavior is in line with what we say about ourselves, people will know what they can depend upon and what they cannot. This can result in the building of trust as people acknowledge our weaknesses, but look to engage with us in our strengths.

Ultimately, definition comes by doing.

Feedback

The second path to self-awareness is noticing what people say about you.

Now, obviously, words are powerful and many of us have had things said to us, especially as children, that were ungenerous, mean, and false. This is not what I am talking about. Instead, I am pointing to potential that others may see in us but to which we ourselves may be blind.

Occasionally, people can be a little surprised when they take The Shapes Test™, especially if the result is not what they expected . . . or hoped for. I've noticed that, in particular, Squares don't want to be Squares, even going as far as asking me to change the name. That's a shame because all Shapes, especially Squares, have extremely valuable attributes—they just don't realize it. Often to our surprise, when we share our results with friends and colleagues, they will agree with the descriptions and even give us examples of where in our lives they see them playing out. If this is the case and if you feel that their answer encapsulates what you believe to be true, I would encourage you to thank people for their words and, by doing so, reinforce them in their minds.

Here is some suggested language to get you started.

If you are a Square:

You will likely be appreciated for your *reliability*.

You could reinforce this by explaining: "You are right, although I don't need fame or the limelight, I really appreciate it when my dependability and dedication are acknowledged. When people recognize how I've assisted them, it helps me if they give me positive feedback on how it helped them. When people acknowledge the benefits of me taking the time to observe and check the correct way of behaving in a situation, it encourages me to go further!"

> "I research to find the obstacles in advance in order to warn people of the wall they are about to hit." — Jim | Square | USA

You might say, "Expect me to want to do things well, but do not expect me to rush things."

If you are a Circle:

You will likely be appreciated for your *sensitivity*.

You could reinforce this by explaining: "It's true, I want to connect on a more authentic level. Therefore, I am sensitive to the needs of others, but I can also be quite sensitive myself. My strength is sometimes my weakness. I interact best in an environment where kind and carefully chosen words are used. I want to take care of and protect others and give special attention to those who give me close and personal attention."

> "If someone is upset, I feel a duty to help them. I see myself as a caregiver. Sometimes poorly chosen words hit harder than some people realize." — Gabe | Brasil | Circle

You might say, "Expect me to take care of and protect others, but also to want others to do the same for me."

If you are a Star:

You will likely be appreciated for your *energy*.

You could reinforce this by explaining: "You nailed it! I think variety is the spice of life and love it when people can keep up with me. I need a chance to laugh, and I don't mind being laughed at as long as people don't mind me laughing at them . . . so, let's laugh together."

> "I try to make things as much fun as possible and try to involve everyone! I wonder, 'How can I change the situation so we can enjoy ourselves?'" — Viveka | India | Star

You might say, "Expect me to get things done, but don't expect me to be all hard work and no play!"

If you are a Triangle:

You will likely be appreciated for your *ingenuity*.

You could reinforce this by explaining: "Yes, I believe that my ideas and vision are significant, and until others see it the same way, I don't mind being the only one who does. I appreciate when people accept that I like to be in control of myself, including my feelings, and that I don't like to be told exactly what to do and how to do it."

> "I bring my ideas to the table with the hope of people recognizing them and therefore being able to use them." — Daniel | Nigeria | Triangle

You might say, "Expect me to create a way forward, but don't expect me to do it the typical way."

Let me encourage you to embrace the best in who people say you are. Don't chase the mirage of who you would rather be, for the sake of greater popularity; it will only lead to you disappointing yourself and others. A healthy self-awareness, clearly defined and backed up by action, will not only help you find your place in this world, but will also help you gain the respect and admiration of others.

To adapt The Serenity Prayer[37] for this purpose, we might ask:

God, grant me the serenity to share the things I cannot change about myself, courage to ask others to challenge me to improve the things I can, and wisdom to know the difference.

The next two chapters cover how to communicate the need for others to assist us with our absent potential, plus how to communicate what we have to give with our evident potential. Clearly, the descriptions I have provided so far in this chapter are just a slice of what you might want to communicate about yourself. You will certainly want to broaden them.

So, what advice can I give you in order to continue that process?

Tips

Here are some suggestions:

1. Define yourself before others do.

    One of the things I have noticed is that if you leave a communication gap, it will often get filled with nonsense. In this context, if you do not define who you are early enough, others may fill in the details and do it for you. The results may not be ideal.

2. Define what makes you unique.

    If you want to be a more interesting communicator, then major on what is distinctive and minor on what is generic. People will listen to you more attentively if you spend less time talking about what is already generally agreed upon and more time on what is different, new, fresh, or unique about what you are saying.

    I'm not sure that many of us do this because, when we asked our research participants to define their personality traits, they often provided descriptions of themselves that were not specific to their Shape, but would be true of most people. For instance:

"I like to help people." Helping others is not unique to anyone's Shape, but the way in which you help them might be. So when you communicate, sharing what makes you different is more likely to stick in their minds.

3. Define what success looks like to you.

    In one of my previous books,[38] I explained that new vision requires new measurements of success. If you are hoping to grow the potential strengths of a particular area of your personality, then make sure that you do not measure your happiness by something else. For instance, if I want to be more courageous and challenge my friends to think more strategically, then I must make sure that I do not measure success by their immediate response. Instead, I should measure it by the growth of those I am assisting in their ability to make great decisions.

4. Define what failure looks like to you.

    A lack of definition may result in people asking you to spend your time on things that are not your strength and therefore hinder your potential. Now, anyone who has lived a little will know that it is unreasonable for us to believe we can spend all our time only doing the things we like to do; there will always be the need for some sort of compromise when working, partnering, or serving with other people. Here is what I have learned: you can compromise on almost everything, except that which made you unique in the first place!

    So, let people know what you can achieve if you are able to play to your strengths, but also do not be afraid to share with them how you might let them down if you are forced to concentrate on your weaknesses. If people trust your motives, they will pivot their expectations.

With this in mind, the ability to define yourself and your potential becomes key to recruiting the kind of people you need in your life and the type of interaction you will want with them. It has been said that "Who you are is who you attract."[39]

I would simply add:

> "Who you say you are is what those you attract will want to help you become."

So, what do the different Shapes have to offer you?

9. The Wisdom of a Fish

How do I share what I need?

Stress

Absent

I had a fantasy.

For many years, I would lie awake at night and dream that, through no fault of my own . . .

The organization I led would fail.

I would imagine any number of reasons for this: maybe the need for my job disappeared; perhaps it was due to a change in the laws governing what I did; or possibly, our non-profit was wiped out by some unforeseen calamity that we could not expect to survive. Whatever the cause, my fantasy dictated that something out of my control would cause me to be set free of my responsibilities, because sometimes I simply could not handle the stress. Although the organization has grown, it has not been smooth. As more people joined us and as our influence has developed, the problems have not disappeared, just altered. The conflicts, disappointments, and burdens I faced twenty-five years ago, now handled by others, have been replaced by larger problems and more complex issues. In the fantasy I described, all of that was taken away from me, and I knew that, for a season at least, I would feel 'at peace.'

I am sure I was not alone.

A number of years ago, my wife turned to me and said:

> "Paul, I thought by now everything would be settled. I thought we would be on top of things and be able to switch to cruise control for the rest of our lives." — The Foxy Lynn | England | Square

That would be nice, wouldn't it? However, the issues will always be with us, and it's rare that every element of life snaps perfectly into place at the same time. The planets rarely align. Even if they do, it's usually only momentary. You may not share the same fantasy as I once did, but we all have things that bring anxiety and the kind of tension that impacts our relationship with one another. After conflict, a major cause of stress in life is said to be when we are forced to operate outside of our talents and gifting—what I would describe as relying on our *absent* potential. Many of these stresses are due to the pressure we put on ourselves; we operate in areas of our weaknesses and then wrestle through them alone. I know that was definitely the case for me when I was younger. Today, however, I feel more energized about what I do than ever before because I have great people around me whose evident abilities underwrite my absent ones.

So how should we communicate our needs to others?

I don't simply mean, how should we tell people our problems, but how do we ask them to come alongside us in the way we actually need? Have you noticed that by trying to help, some people actually make things worse? This is because they offer the kind of help that they themselves would need but do not provide the kind of assistance we ourselves really want. And it's our fault! Why? Because as I said earlier, if we leave a communication gap, it usually gets filled with nonsense.

To harness the strengths of others, there are two things to bear in mind:

1. It is vital that we recognize and admit that we struggle.

2. We must communicate exactly what we hope to get from them.

Let's see how understanding our Shapes can aid us in both of these areas.

Indicators

Stress can come in different forms for the different Shapes.

I cannot speak to everyone's individual pressure points, of course, but let me share with you the tensions that generally affect each personality type. Through this, I hope to give you the words to express yourself as well as the affirmation that doing so is no bad thing!

Similar to our demotivators, our stress points can have negative results on our relationships. But, unlike our demotivators, the indicators I am about to give are the ones we create ourselves. They are the result of a personality type operating in isolation.

As a Square, you may feel the strain of *unrealistic expectations*.

> The problem with feeling responsible is that, although you aim to take on only what you can do well, your desire to serve can trump your cautiousness and cause you to take on too much. A desire to fulfill the expectations of others can lead you to take on extra things that can then overwhelm you, especially if the time restraints are ambiguous or hasty. Instead of a group of friends using a stretcher to carry a responsibility, you may put all that weight into your own backpack and carry a burden too heavy for one person to bear. This has a tendency to push you into areas where you don't feel supported and instead face *insecurity, instability*, and *lack of structure* that may frighten you.
>
>> "I try to do everything very well, and I want to do the things I said we would. If I see I can't do them, then I worry and I feel ashamed." — Anne | Germany | Square

If you allow self-pity to rise to the top, you may end up taking out your frustration on the very people you intended to serve.

Your stress indicators may be:

> You lash out at those you love the most.
>
> You feel unreasonable levels of guilt.
>
> Your attitude reflects doom and gloom, and you struggle to see a hopeful outcome.
>
> Physically, your appetite and ability to sleep may suffer.

As a Circle, you may be concerned by the *pursuit of targets*.

> You see the health of your relationships with others as vital and may feel uncomfortable when goals and objectives appear to be more important to them than your well-being or the well-being of others. This is especially true if you sense a lack of emotional support. Language is important to you, and you are more susceptible to the negative effects of *sarcasm*, *ridicule*, and *poorly chosen words* that can arise in a pressurized relationship.
>
>> "Enforcing rules on someone who is having a hard time seems harsh and is hard for me to do. I really just want to be there for the person." — Mike | USA | Circle
>
> Without realizing it, you may focus more on the emotion behind things said and done to you than the actual words or actions themselves. You may get so caught up in your own feelings that if you succumb to oversensitivity, then ironically, this might lead you to become insensitive in your words and actions towards others.
>
> Your stress indicators may be:
>
>> You cry or get upset easily and are unsure why.
>>
>> You space out.
>>
>> You create an imaginary world where hopes and dreams are preferred over reality.

Physically, you may develop stomach aches or mild feelings of ill health.

As a Star, you may struggle with the *fear of failure*.

You want to get things done, and sometimes you can get a little ahead of yourself. Your enthusiasm and sense of confidence can cause you to rush ahead without waiting for others to catch up, which leaves you a little isolated. When things are going well, that's fine, but if they start to break down, then this can develop into an acute sense of *anger*, *frustration*, and *fear of failure*, resulting in unresolved issues with the people or circumstances that let you down.

> "When I don't get the right support, I can't sit still. I try to get away from the stress and then may come back to the situation later." — Paul | India | Star

Your frustrations can lead to feelings of anger and disappointment towards those who you feel failed to give you the kind of enthusiastic support you wanted. They may have warned you about the possible problems and accuse you of not listening. If under stress, your response to this could appear somewhat abusive and overbearing.

Your stress indicators may be:

A tendency to rant and rave.

Feeling hamstrung by perceived abandonment leading to restless frustration.

Your behavior is perceived as intimidating or menacing.

Physically, you may have a hard time sitting still and be unable to relax or switch off.

As a Triangle, you may struggle with *lack of control*.

You have high expectations of how things should be, and your modus operandi might be to deconstruct and reconstruct, pulling things down in order to then rebuild them better. At times, this may lead you to over-analyze a situation or relationship. In life, it is always easier to deconstruct than construct, and you may find that you have dismantled something without then being able to rebuild it. Faced with an impasse, and unable to find a solution, feelings of *doubt*, *confusion*, and *powerlessness* may set in and disable you.

> "Sometimes, I can feel indecisive or take longer to make decisions. I get hung up looking at the pros and cons of every single thing. I look at all the variables to decide." — Lathan | USA | Triangle

Few on the outside may see it, but on the inside you may resemble a toddler sitting on the floor sobbing his heart out because he has torn apart a Lego set and now realizes he is unable to put it back together again.

Your stress indicators may be:

> Becoming prone to obsessive and compulsive behavior.
>
> A tendency to non-conformity that may become unreasonable.
>
> Using wit and wisdom to put people down.
>
> Physically, you may stumble in your language or find it hard to think straight.

If you noticed earlier, I said I *had* a fantasy, not I *have* a fantasy.

As my primary Shape is a Triangle and my secondary Shape a Star,[40] I believe that what was really bothering me was a fear of failing to prove my ideas would work. I'm convinced that what I do is important and imperative; it feels more like a calling than a career. Added to my introverted nature and tendency to keep my emotions to myself, I now realize that I was putting everything on my own shoulders.

I needed to open up, and as I did, I found it easier to ask others to come alongside me and inject their various types of support into the work I was doing.

Upon absorbing their influence, I then needed to learn the wisdom of a fish.

Equilibrium

In 1997, I qualified as a Sports Diver with the British Sub-Aqua Club of Great Britain.

It took me a year of biology lessons and underwater excursions. I've learned that, due to the weight and pressure of water, the deeper I dive, the more I am in danger. As the pressure builds, the less mobile I feel. The longer I am down, the more time is required to come up to the surface because of the changes in my body. In fact, at certain depths, human beings need submarines to cope with that pressure, and the lower they go, the thicker their walls need to be. Annoyingly, when you are in the depths, moving slowly and somewhat awkwardly, you notice the irritating agility of the fish that swim around you. They come up to your mask and dart away in the blink of an eye. They scurry with ease across the seafloor, disappearing within seconds the minute you slowly reach out to touch them.

How?

Equilibrium - a stable state characterized by the cancellation of all forces by equal opposing forces.

It's simple. The pressure inside of a fish is equal to the pressure out-side of it. This helped me realize that you and I have a choice when it comes to our reaction to the pressures in life and the stresses we must undergo. We can either cope in the same way a submarine does, just building thicker and thicker skin until the inevitable implo-sion takes place, or aspire to the wisdom of a fish and ensure that whatever is within us is equal to the pressure outside of us.

The key to adopting the wisdom of a fish is to recognize the type of pressure we are under in order to find the appropriate response. If I am under mental stress due to constantly creating new teaching material, I need to pursue equilibrium by building up my mental capacity with reading, watching, and listening to the material that will boost my creativity. However, if I am under physical duress, then reading more books will not help; instead, I must exercise and focus on my diet. The pressure of finding innovative solutions to strategic problems requires yet another type of discipline whereby I must find the time to meditate and exercise myself spiritually. Of course, in all of this, relationships are key. Importantly, if I'm under emotional pressure from challenging and supporting people in their journey, I need to spend as much time building relationships with people who will look after me as I spend with those I am helping. All of this requires a level of vulnerability. However, that is only half of the battle. I also need to equip my friends with understanding *how* I need to receive their help.

Allowing people in so that they can both encourage and challenge us can be an awkward process. Real relationships have a habit of cutting through the veneer. Let's look at why each Shape may struggle with this process and how we can communicate in such a way that those helping us know how to provide us with the kind of help we really need as opposed to the kind of help they think we need.

Here is some advice on what to know and share.

If you are a Square:

> You may find yourself in a catch-22 situation. Squares are typically a little guarded, especially if someone loses their confidence. You may only open up when you really trust someone, and yet to trust someone new, you must rub away the veneer to see if that person is truly trustworthy. Although you may prefer to sit back and observe a person to find out if they are dependable, building deeper relationships in which someone else can bring

out the best in us often requires that we first give something of ourselves away—a secret, an insecurity, a hope, a fear—all in order to discover whether that new person can be responsible with it. And so, here's the catch—we have to trust people in order to build our trust in them!

"I've had to learn to ignore past betrayals in order not to ruin future relationships." — Emily | USA | Square

For many Squares, once bitten, twice shy. If you have been let down by someone in the past (as we all have), you may be more prone than other Shapes to keep to yourself the very things you need to give away. Sadly, you may worry that the vulnerability required is too high a risk. However, when you do allow people to help you grow, here are a few phrases that you might want to use:

"Please don't use harsh words; I'm already my own worst critic!"

"Please give me firm structures I can rely upon."

"Please let me know what you expect and what you don't expect of me."

"Please share the plan well ahead of time to let me process."

"Please show me rather than just tell me."

"Please reassure me if I am doing this right . . . I need to feel secure."

"I don't mind if you question me; just do it at the appropriate time."

If you are a Circle:

Your lower than average conflict threshold is problematic because it is impossible to rub away the veneer without some level of friction. We don't really know someone until we know where we disagree with them, and we may not have a true friend until we've come through conflict with our relationship still intact. So, although friction may lead you to believe that a person could never offer the level of relationship you seek, it may be exactly what is required to get that friendship to where you want it to be. Although this removal of the veneer may at times feel too abrasive, the process is right, but you may feel it is going wrong . . . and walk away.

> "I desire deeper relationships, but conflict is something I both fear and get frustrated with. As I tend to stray away from it, it has become an obstacle to better friendships." — Megan | USA | Circle

One of the difficulties we have noticed is that, although Circles are great at connecting emotionally with people, the communication of their thoughts may not always be clear. You likely have a deep internal conversation and, without realizing it, you often expect people to feel what you want to say with the same level of intuition that you possess. Therefore, when you do speak, what you say can be a little abstract, unclear, or even confusing. Here are some things you might want to tell others in order to give them a heads up:

> "Please understand that talking about feelings and problems is helpful to me."

> "Please do not be frightened away by my tears and emotion."

> "Using my name and remembering details about me help me trust you."

> "If you want me to open up, I need to know your hopes and dreams."

> "I respond best when we collaborate to resolve a problem."

> "Please show me you understand how I feel about the issue."

> "Please give me your undivided attention; if you are distracted, I will check out."

If you are a Star:

As much as you really appreciate the input of others, you trust your gut instinct. You are not looking for someone to tell you what to do; instead, you are hoping they will help you find your own answer. It is not that you don't like to collaborate with others; you do. However, you want your friends, colleagues, and family to be independent. You hope they will concentrate on the things that they are responsible for while allowing you space to work on whatever you are working on.

> "I don't like step-by-step anything. I had to assemble a desk one time and I didn't like it. I don't need people to tell me exactly what to do; instead, I like to be presented with a challenge. If I don't complete the goal, then sure, I failed, but ultimately I compete against myself!" — Isaac | USA | Star

Stars tend to keep things a little light. You likely want your relationships to be fun, exciting, and not 'too heavy.' You want to move fast and may not want to get bogged down in the excessive drama that relationships can bring. You don't mind people being direct, but you want to solve a problem quickly and move on. However, some people won't, will they? They may want to spend time working through problems and issues; they may want to go over the same ground time and again, which you might find somewhat irritating. You may not have an issue with some of the friction that creates an authentic relationship, but you may find it takes too long . . . and be tempted to skip it! To help people help you, you might want to let them know:

> "Please don't try to change me; instead, try to challenge me."

> "From time to time, I need to vent, but please don't take it personally."

> "Please feel free to be blunt; I don't mind as long as I can be forthright in return."

"If you have advice or a challenge, I'll respond better if you share it with enthusiasm!"

"The more fun it will be, the more engaged I will be . . . and for longer."

"I want to party but to party with a purpose!"

"If we do something active when collaborating, that would be cool!"

If you are a Triangle:

Triangles can appear somewhat emotionless because they tend to wear their brain on their sleeve rather than their heart. You may be happy to express yourself and express what you are feeling but prefer to be in control of how you display that emotion. Essentially, you may be more comfortable sharing your emotions than showing them. You are therefore happy to talk about ideas, but 'excessive' conversations centered around feelings and emotions may make you uncomfortable.

"Sometimes people don't understand logic, especially my sibling. I tell them I don't want the drama, just give me your reasoning." — Shilisha | India | Triangle

The problem, of course, is that ideas and thoughts are not enough to build an authentic relationship. In fact, people will rarely buy into your vision of what you hope to become until they've bought into your story. You feel it is important that they know what you know, but they may be more interested in knowing what you feel. It's awkward, and so, for you, friction comes when people expect a level of intimacy you are not willing to share. You may struggle to invite them into your deeper feelings. Although you understand the importance of removing the veneer in your relationships, you might think it is too intrusive. As you ignore this perceived over-stepping of the mark, people may feel excluded and withdraw their help and support. In order to keep them engaged, here are some phrases that may help:

> "Although I rarely express my needs, it does not mean I don't have them."
>
> "If I do share my need with you, it's probably more serious than I make it sound."
>
> "Please listen to my ideas; they are very important to me."
>
> "I love questions; if you use them, you will keep me engaged."
>
> "I may not express myself emotionally, but I can still be hurt."
>
> "Please understand that when I make a suggestion . . . it's not just a suggestion."
>
> "I respond best to criticism when it is given in a matter-of-fact, non-dramatic way."

The sooner you decide to communicate your needs . . . the sooner you will wonder why you never did it before! However, as much as sharing our burdens is important, we cannot hope that our friends, employers, or family can remove them. In the book, *Future Leader*, by Dr. Viv Thomas, the author pointed to a future where organizations would no longer be perceived as a parent by its employees.[41] This is proving true. In the past, many people were given jobs for life, and the world seemed a more secure place. People were less transient and communities were more likely to know you and offer you stronger support. Yet the world has changed, and therefore, more than ever, we must be more proactive when we take care of ourselves and one another. With that in mind, I would like to share some generic tips that I have found helpful in dealing with my own stress over the last thirty years.

Tips

I hope the following will be of some benefit to you.

1.   I have made some personal commitments to myself.

131

Importantly, for me, most of them are connected to my work. Here are a few I made many years ago: I have made peace with the fact that my work is a lifestyle and have taken personal responsibility for my mental and emotional health. I take a full day off each week when I actively try not to think about work and limit work-related messages. I ensure I have close friends outside of my workplace. I take all my vacation time and enjoy it. I have at least one lifetime interest outside my work that I enjoy at least once a week. I am currently involved in learning about something that has nothing to do with my work. I take the initiative to talk about other things than work with my colleagues. My spouse and children have my attention when I am spending quality time with them.

2. I focus on the climate rather than the weather.

    If I plan a vacation ahead of time and I want to find out the likelihood of the weather in a certain part of the world, I don't check the weather in that place on the day because the weather on the day I am booking is no indication of what may be happening months or even a week from now. Instead, I find out the general climate for the place during the time of year that I am planning to visit. In a similar way, I have learned not to get caught up in the feelings of the day but to step back and look at the 'climate of my emotions' over a season. Focusing on my momentary feelings each day has resulted in a helter-skelter of emotions that will not only drive me crazy, but also cause me to put those I relate to under stress.

    In focusing on the climate, I often find that things are not as bad as I think they are. If, however, they are, then I will reach out for more help.

3. I've learned to think about how I feel and vice versa.

    One of my problems is that I'm so busy thinking about what I am doing and how to improve it, that I forget to enjoy how it feels when it is going well. If what I am doing is going badly, I've learned to stop and ask myself how I am feeling—something I never used to do. Recognizing that I am a little down can make me aware of how I might treat people around me and remind me to get whatever kind of equilibrium I need at the time.

4. I take a little time out to enjoy the fruits of any success.

    Reward yourself. Ideally, do it with those you had the success with. Simple as that.

5. Recognize that the grass is often tinged with yellow on the other side.

    Working with young adults has highlighted to me the tendency for people to constantly be thinking about the next thing rather than relaxing in what they are doing right now. Added to that, those who are still developing their emotional maturity and understanding of how life really works sometimes misread a relationship that is going through a difficult patch—a.k.a. rubbing away veneer—as a bad relationship. Then, imagining that other relationships will be perfect, they wander off. At times like these, it is helpful to remember the following proverb:

    > "Don't throw away the water you are carrying because you see a mirage!" — Anonymous

    Occasionally, a person very different from me, with whom I have had an awkward relationship at first, has turned out to be a real benefit and blessing in my life. So, sticking with them but communicating how I'd like their input has been a great step forward.

For many of us who hope to do something good in the world, life can feel like we are walking on a tightrope where one small gust of wind can be the difference between success and failure. Playing on our minds can be that one small thing which, should it go wrong, might cause everything to fall apart. Yet simultaneously, we know that there is another little thing that, should it go right, could lead to a wonderful breakthrough. I'm hoping that something in this chapter may have helped you when feeling the stresses and strains of that tension. In particular, I hope you have learned a little more about how to communicate what you might need from others.

Now, how can you share what you would like to give?

10. Social Reality

How do I share what I have to give?

Influence

Math

It's no good having something good to offer if no one knows it's being offered!

In his TED talk, *How YouTube is Driving Innovation*, the curator of one of the world's most influential conferences, Chris Anderson, encourages us to activate the dormant talent within our society by moving from one-to-many to many-to-many. He unpacks an online movement whereby innovation comes when we move beyond one person teaching a group to a culture where friends, neighbors, and whole communities motivate and influence one another.

The power of this for good or bad is quite surprising, especially when you start doing the math. I once read of a calculation that can be used to figure out the number of connections in a group of people. Each connection (or relationship) is a potential catalyst for something great. The number of connections is equal to the number of people times itself, minus that same original number, and then divided by two. As an equation, I am told it looks something like this:

$$R = (N^2 - N) \div 2$$

So, in a room of 2 people, there is 1 relationship. In a room of 3 people, there are 3 relationships. In a room of 5 people, there are 10 relationships. Yet as a crowd builds, something magical happens;

the possibilities grow exponentially. In a room of 100 people, there are 4,950 different relationships!

Can you imagine the benefit of activating the positive influence of 4,950 relationships?!

> "What if, in the coming crowd of nine billion, that crowd could learn enough to be net contributors, instead of net plunderers? That changes everything, right? I mean, that would take more teachers than we've ever had. But the good news is they are out there . . . Who's the teacher? You're the teacher!"42 — Chris Anderson, Curator of the TED Conferences

Although our communities have this potential, I would like to add to Anderson's observation that if we do not harness the benefits of many-to-many to bring something good into our world, others may use this dynamic in order to bring something bad. I am all about many-to-many, and much of my working life has been dedicated to activating this potential, especially in young people. However, in every generation I see a clear obstacle in the form of poor communication, both internally and externally.

Let me explain.

Internally, when recognizing the *latent* potential in a friend, neighbor, or colleague and considering the idea of offering to help them, do you ask, "Who do I think I am to suggest this?" Or perhaps, "What makes me so great?" Might you talk yourself out of helping people in this way?

Externally, I am very aware that, if we offer to collaborate with others by 'promoting' our *evident* potential, we *may* expose ourselves to all manner of criticism—especially since helping others become the best they can be involves giving criticism, an ugly word in our hyper-sensitive world. The different personalities complicate this even further. Our well-intentioned positivity can be perceived poorly due to the different ways in which the Shapes communicate their thoughts and feelings. If we don't do a good job of making ourselves understood, each Shape has the ability to come across badly.

If you are a Square, you might be perceived as being *bossy*.

> Squares know that if something is worth doing it should be done right, but your pursuit of putting the right foundation into place might seem overbearing. The danger is that others may misinterpret your intentions as dictatorial and miss out on all that you have to offer.

If you are a Circle, your attempts may appear *naive*.

> Circles look for the positive in people, which may come across as a little sycophantic. A desire to pursue a common goal in close relational proximity might be seen by some as a little smothering. This is a shame because, when you really connect with a person, you truly commit to them and their ambitions.

If you are a Star, you may come across as *foolhardy*.

> Stars tend to be impulsive, which can be interpreted as not thinking things through. Your positive demeanor might even intimidate someone with a more cautious attitude. This is unfortunate because what you offer can be hugely effective as a catalyst for action.

If you are a Triangle, you might be accused of *arrogance*.

> Triangles tend to base everything on a theory or principle that they have personally bought into. This fixation on communicating the 'why' can lead others to believe you are patronizing or that you perhaps see them as a little 'simple.' Sadly, people may push away from your great ideas as they misinterpret your conviction for self-importance.

For many-to-many to happen, we all need to make our *evident* potential available. Yet, understandably, you might feel awkward approaching a friend, colleague, or neighbor to offer them your advice or even yourself as a role model.

So, how can you communicate in a way that people bite off your hand, not your head?

Numbers

First, please don't back away; we need you!

For us to activate our potential and realize our goals, we need your input more than we may ever realize. If you remember, I said earlier that as a general rule I rarely share my goals publicly. I also mentioned that declaring a target has a terrible habit of derailing our ability to achieve it. Repeated psychology tests[43] since 1926 have proven this time and time again.

Here's why . . .

In one of the most recent examinations of the subject, 163 people across four separate tests were asked to write down their goals. Half of them were asked to verbally share their goal with the rest of the group, and the other half were told they could not. Both groups were then given a specific amount of time to list all they would need to do in order to fulfill their targets. Worryingly, the group that had shared their hopes and dreams publicly created their list without taking all the available time. However, those who were in the group that was kept quiet requested an extension because they felt they had much more planning to do.

So what?

Researchers say this is an example of what they refer to as 'Social Reality,' whereby freely and repeatedly telling others your vision gives you a false sense that it has been completed. You get the buzz of victory as though you've already achieved something! Sadly, this often results in a loss of impetus to do the real work required to accomplish your objectives. This effect is seen in various experiments where those who share their goals publicly appear less motivated and less able to imagine all that they need to do in order to accomplish their vision. Essentially, sharing your goal lulls you into a false sense of success!

Unless . . .

You have people to help keep you accountable and push you forward. If people have someone to walk alongside them in order to help them do what needs to be done, goal-setting transitions from a negative to a positive tool.

The great news is that being 'the teacher,' as Anderson calls it, does not require you to have all the answers. That's fine because, to get started, all you really need is one question—a question you can ask of the person you want to collaborate with: "Can you see the potential that I see in you?" What everyone needs is someone who believes in them and is willing to come alongside them to bring out their best. In fact, this reminds me to ask you a question:

Have you noticed the irony yet?

Don't you think it's a little odd that a Triangle is writing a book about connecting with others? Surely, a Circle should be doing this, right? Yet the required ability to create The Shapes Test™, a tool to help people connect with each other, is not the skill of connecting with people. Rather than calling for an intuitive heart, it calls for a strategic mind. Importantly, we don't have to be that much better than those we help at whatever it is we want to help them with. I realized this at an early age when I was surprised to learn that top athletes had coaches. Surely, I thought to myself, the person who teaches a tennis player how to play tennis must be a better tennis player than the one they are teaching. Of course, I was wrong. What an Olympian needs is not someone who is better than them at what they do, but someone who has the ability to recognize and grow their *latent* potential.

Are you willing to rise to that challenge?

Language

What this book hopes to supply more than anything else is language—in particular, language that enables you to express yourself in a way that avoids the problem of people misunderstanding or misinterpreting your offer of help. So, allow me the privilege of offering you some suggestions according to your Shape.

As a Square, you may want to offer your *loyalty*.

> You might say: "I see myself as an armor-bearer."

"I want to support you in the best way possible, and so please forgive me if I come across as a little authoritarian. It's just that it's very important to me that I do everything exactly as we have agreed, on time, and correctly. I'm sorry if this may come across as though I am telling you what to do, but in reality, I'm doing it because I really need you to tell me exactly what you expect of me. Getting clear instructions from you allows me to assist you the right way . . . I would hate to let you down!"

> "My worst fear is dropping the ball, forgetting something, and not following through!" — Stephanie | USA | Square

Here's a list of phrases you might use:

> "I will be here for you; don't worry, I'm not going to leave you in a mess."

> "I can create the systems and routines that will help you."

> "I can help you research what you need to know."

> "I can provide consistency as I'm good with checkups and checklists."

> "I can keep guard of the traditions that you value."

> "I can be a devoted partner; just give me something to believe in."

"I'm great at keeping confidences . . . You can be confident in that!"

As a Circle, you may want to offer your *company.*

You might say: "I see myself as a confidante."

"I may look to the stars at times and perhaps come across as a little naive in my expectations for you, but that is just because I like to wear my heart on my sleeve. It is important for us to take the time to express our hopes and dreams with each other because in this way, although I know we may not achieve every-thing we speak of, I believe it will inspire and connect us. I hope that we will always take a collaborative approach to the chal-lenges we face together because I see your challenges as my challenges."

"Telling others my weaknesses and insecurities creates an invitation into which they can share their own vulnerabilities. We can then journey together." — Murph | USA | Circle

Here's a list of words you might use:

"I can help you discover how you feel about what you are doing."

"I can help you feel what other people are feeling."

"I can help you communicate with others on an emotional level."

"I can give you lots of personal attention."

"I can bring you emotional support if you open up and make time for me."

"I'm good at keeping in contact and enjoy sending encourag-ing messages."

"I love to dream and I'm happy to spend time imagining great possibilities."

As a Star, you may want to offer your *enthusiasm*.

You might say: "I see myself as a cheerleader."

"I love momentum and see our relationship as a potential adventure. I know I might sometimes appear a little reckless, but I understand that to grow we first have to give things a go! I like to be active and want to help you remove obstacles and move forward. I can see the positives in the issues we may face, and I want to help you see them too!"

> "We are not a Shape to back down when something challenges us. Other Shapes might crumble, but we explode!" — Chloe | England | Star

Here's a list of words you might use:

> "I like to fix things and would love to help you as you problem-solve!"
>
> "I like to find positive solutions where we can both prosper."
>
> "If we feel we need to go a new direction, I'll be okay with that!"
>
> "When we hit a problem, don't worry, it won't put me off!"
>
> "I'd love to bring my certain set of practical and pragmatic skills."
>
> "I'm a self-starter and I'm definitely not needy!"
>
> "I'll encourage you to celebrate when you achieve something great!"

As a Triangle, you may want to offer your *ideas*.

You might say: "I see myself as a trailblazer!"

"Please understand that I process by sharing my ideas. I know it might appear that I think I know everything, but in reality I know that not everything I think of will work. I'm just trying out my ideas to see if they do. I want to help my world become a better place, and so I look for new principles and patterns to life . . . Once I discover them, I believe passing them on is the best way I can help those I care about. In saying that, I prefer not to force my opinions on others but to be invited to share them."

"I rarely offer myself or my advice unless I am first asked. I hope I am." — Alex | Syria | Triangle

Here's a list of words you might use:

"When things become chaotic, I can bring a calming influence."

"I can arbitrate for you if you need an objective opinion."

"I won't try to be more popular than you; I just want to be influential."

"I will help you think through a plan from different angles."

"I can help you know how to think, not just what to think."

"I'd love to help you communicate your ideas to others!"

"The more I can explain, the more practical my advice becomes."

Endorsing the unrealized possibilities you see in your friend is a powerful first step in the battle of good over evil, and learning how to communicate what you want to give makes your proposal more likely to succeed! Of course, positive language driven by a genuine love for people covers a multitude of communication sins. Did you know that according to recent research, you are far more likely to be viewed favorably if your social media posts are positive—even if people disagree with you? Plus, you are more likely to be viewed unfavorably if your social media posts are negative, even if those who read them sympathize with you![44]

"Kind words can be short and easy to speak, but their echoes are truly endless."[45] — Mother Teresa

More than ever before, people value someone who will bring a positive influence into their lives.

Tips

When people say yes to your offer of help, here are my tips for collaboration:

1.   Don't throw your pearls to the pigs.

     As much as I am encouraging you to offer your help to others, never offer it to those who don't want it. I would encourage you to 'Spread' the message that you want to help people. 'Spot' those looking for help. 'Stay' with them while they are still keen to learn. Then, 'Send' those same people to those who did not respond to you. I talk more about this process in my book, *Shalom: How to Reach Anyone Anywhere.*[46] Furthermore, if I no longer believe in someone's commitment to an objective, I stop challenging them. Carrying on will only exasperate them, frustrate me, and waste all of our time!

2.   Listen to what they really need.

     My English friend, Kevin, moved to the States a few years before I did and gave me some simple but time-saving advice. After several years of having to clarify himself over the phone, either to government agencies, restaurant staff, or store employees, he explained:

     > "They are not listening to you; they're first trying to figure out where you are from."

     It was true. The first 30 seconds were pointless and so, on his advice, I learned to chat with people about nonessentials—the weather, their day, the news, whatever! Only after this brief buffer, do I now share what I really want to communicate. In the same way, when you approach someone, don't jump in thinking that, because you can see their potential, this is all that's needed. You first need to know if they see their potential and, if so, where they feel they need help.

3. Build on joint objectives.

    Once you have listened to people, find a joint objective. Never try to force someone into a goal that they do not believe in, nor try to help someone with a goal you do not believe that they can achieve. Instead, find something you can honestly commit to and make a note of it.

    Also, you might need to recalibrate your relationship slightly. In the past, you perhaps only encouraged each other, but now that you know you want to go on a deeper journey, you may have to lay out some new ground rules. You might want to clearly outline the levels of encouragement and criticism you are both willing to give and receive.

4. Build on shared credit.

    I once read of a great rule when partnering with someone. Again, it came down to the use of language, and it went something like this:

    > If we succeed: "You did it."
    >
    > If we do okay: "We did it."
    >
    > If we fail: "I did it."

    Infusing relationships with this mantra at the appropriate times and on a regular basis will help you create goodwill, especially if you are seen as the one leading the relationship.

5. The more *specific* it is, the more *dynamic* it will be.

    When it comes to words of encouragement, can I encourage you to major in the details?

    With encouragement, rather than simply telling someone they did a great job, tell them exactly what they did that was so great. The sentence, "You did that well," is not as powerful or as strong as, "I noticed how you made sure everyone had exactly what they needed; your research was impeccable."

With criticism: "You made them feel terrible!" is just not helpful at all. What would be more beneficial is: "Whenever they wanted to share their thoughts and feelings with you, you broke eye contact, looked around, and probably made them feel their ideas were insignificant."

6. Make a commitment and then stick to it.

    Can I encourage you to stick with people on whatever journey you go on together? When it comes to 'real' relationships, the kind that take time to build, we have to ask ourselves: Am I a sticky note or a postage stamp? A sticky note is used to share little messages and is very easy to peel away with any kind of force that pulls at it. A postage stamp, however, provides authenticity and sticks to something until it eventually gets there.

    Nothing of any value happens in a moment, and the kind of community that we all hope for takes time to build. Without investing that time, our relationships will be superficial and too easy to walk away from; but with it, they will give us the strength to do the special things we may have in our hearts to build.

This book has been simply an introduction to all that can be learned. I have much more to share when it comes to applying our research to couples, parents, teams, schools, churches, charitable organizations, and businesses. Yet, uniting them all is an underlying motive which I would like to leave with you.

Us

During the writing of this book, one of my biggest encouragers passed away at seventy-seven years old. Her name was Henny. When I was younger, and others may have doubted my hopes and dreams, she would often raise her thumbs and tell me to, "Go for it!" Years later when my family and I left for the USA, she would constantly 'like' and comment on almost every post I made on social media, telling me to keep moving forward, celebrating any success, posting encouraging messages she felt might help. My wife and I nicknamed her 'The Facebook Queen.' She was my online stalker. We were not the only ones who saw her in this light; in fact, she was so keen to encourage people that she would sometimes 'like' things that, as a pastor's wife, she probably should not have . . . much to everyone's amusement! The theory was that sometimes she never actually read everything she gave the thumbs up to and so, to test that theory, a friend decided to post a picture of an orange to see if Henny would 'like' it. Nothing else, no comment or explanation, just a photo of a random orange.

Sure enough, Henny gave it a digital thumbs up!

When she passed away, a friend of mine made an insightful comment:

> "Henny 'liked' something not because she liked the post, but because she liked you!"

Earlier in the book, I encouraged you to let your love for others drive your goals. Henny was an encourager. I don't know her Shape. It's not that important. What she will be remembered for is not her personality type, but how she used her personality and talents for the good of others. This is also the aim of The Shapes Test™. As I said in the very first chapter, this tool is not an exercise in navel-gazing; it aims to go beyond helping us simply understand ourselves or each other. Nor is the end goal to aid us as we make ourselves better understood. Instead, the hope is that what we have learned here will equip and enable us to build something good together.

I may not be as intuitive as many of my readers when it comes to building relationships, and that's okay because my primary aim is not to connect with my readers, but to mobilize my readers to connect with each other.

As I said earlier, I believe in you, but more than that . . .

I believe in us.

4

What are my next steps and how was The Shapes Test™ created?

A1. The Shape of Things to Come

What can I do next?

Next Steps

If you find this book helpful, here are some suggestions for what you might want to do next. All of the following resources can be found at TheShapesTest.com.

Receive the MyShapes newsletter

Videos, stories, and new research will provide new information about your Shape. Go to TheShapestTest.com.

Discover your Shape's Weight

You can go online to The Shapes Test™ website and, for a donation towards our work with young people, discover the order of your Shapes and their percentage based on your test results. This proves helpful when discovering why and how, in certain circumstances and with certain people, your other Shapes might kick into action.

Complete the MyShapes Journal

This simple tool will guide you to get the most out of The Shapes Test™ and turn what you've learned into action. Find it wherever books are sold.

Read other books based on The Shapes Test™

Future books include *The Team Shapes*, *The Couple Shapes*, *The Parent Shapes*, and more.

Book a Masterclass

Fun, interactive, and practical, these presentations come in all shapes and sizes and are ideal for your business, party, school, neighborhood group, church, conference, or creative event. Choose from various licensed trainers with up-to-date information. Go to TheShapesTest.com.

A2. The Formation of 'The Shapes Test™'

How was the test created?

Science

The Shapes Test™ builds upon the work of others.

In ancient Greece, the physician Hippocrates believed that people could be divided into four temperaments, namely: Sanguine, Phlegmatic, Choleric, and Melancholic. Known as the Father of Western Medicine, Hippocrates' theory was based on his medical insight. His thoughts on bodily fluids known as 'humors' were used to create the now-famous four personality types. Although much of what he wrote regarding the biological reasoning behind them did not stand the test of time, his ideas on the four indicators did. Plus, they inspired further work on the subject.

One hundred years ago, the Swiss psychiatrist Carl Jung, who founded analytical psychology, further researched the idea of four personality types using clinical observation. Transitioning from Hippocrates' scientific terms, he replaced them with the more user-friendly words: Thinking, Feeling, Sensation, Intuition. He also added another two distinctives for each of the four traits, namely, 'extraverted' and 'introverted,' thus presenting eight types.

Inspired by Jung's book, during World War 2, the Myers-Briggs personality type indicator was developed to help women entering the workplace identify the sort of war-time jobs that would be the most comfortable and effective for them. Their work aimed to give society a pragmatic application to understanding personality types. Again, adding more layers, Katharine Cook Briggs and her daughter, Isabel Briggs Myers, created sixteen personality indicators providing each one with a title summarized by four letters.

Since then, there have been various other works on the subject, some simply inspired by the four personality types and some directly based upon them, some serious and some just for fun. The common denominator is that, whereas Myers-Briggs sought a pragmatic application, they branched off into more specific applications, such as Love Languages for Couples, StrengthsFinder (now Clifton Strengths) used to recognize talents, and True Colors, originally introduced to me as a tool for children. Added to these are the almost infinite number of fun tests that have become so popular on social media platforms.

For reasons that I have explained in the first chapter of this book, The Shapes Test™ has built upon what went before it in order to create 'one test to rule them all'—a simple tool for the more generic goal of creating a language that everyone can remember, understand, and use in all of their relationships. The Shapes Test™ employs a purposely simpler test with an emphasis on pragmatic relational wisdom. Additionally, it involves research that was carried out through presentations, feedback, analysis, and surveys with for-profits, non-profits, neighborhood groups, family groups, churches, youth groups, and online platforms. Constantly tweaking these results over many years, with research beginning in 2004, The Shapes Test™ was finally created in its present format during the COVID-19 pandemic, and this first book was written during the lockdown of 2020.

We hope it helps.

A3. Special Mentions

Who helped with the research?

Thanks

Collectives

A big thank you to the thousands of people who have participated in The Shape Test™ presentations including its previous formats. To those whose interaction and feedback helped me and my team refine, re-analyze, and reproduce the material within this book. To the businesses, churches, neighborhood groups, organizations, and other agencies that opened the doors for us to connect with their people for the purpose of conducting surveys both informally and formally.

A special thank you to Richard Taylor and the team at ISARC for their expertise in developing The Shapes Test™ software. isarc.co.uk

Individuals

A special mention to those who contributed quotes or explanations of their Shapes that were particularly helpful in shaping my understanding of their personality type, many of which were included in the book.

The Squares:

Ronaldo Andrade. Stephanie Rogers. Emily Tutton. Jim Sorenson. Anne Weinmann. Lynn Gibbs. Sara Wilhite. Ashley Lytle. Wendy Sager. Rebecca Lamprecht. Gabriel Greinert. Courtney Jansz. Sara Kliever.

Raphael Nyatuame. Relie Nyatuame. Samuel Amasah. Matheus Santos. Neander Goforth. Praveen Salam. Christine Bohlin. Sonya Griffith. Stephanie Smith.

The Circles:

Michael Murphy. Courtney Walsh. Sakhawat Masih. Taylor Walsh. David Panzer. Megan Freiwald. Paige Tighe. Mike Sherrill. Terry Harris. Sean Sebastian. Mark Scott. Felix Schneider. Keren Johnson. Clement Prince. Pete Baker. Gabriel Andrade. Shannon Schmid.

The Stars:

Leonard Browning. Matthew Powell. Drea Taylor. Reuben Williams. Kim Walsh. Viveka Rajesh. Elena Hild. Sruthika Kandakatla. Andy Clark. Vilma Albey. Jamie Flores. Hugh Sager. Isaac Washington. Bethan Steele. Melissa Neves. Paul Augustine. John Wesley. Chloe Povey. Jonny Borst. Tobias Müller. Portia Nnuro.

The Triangles:

Alexandra Swires-Murphy. Carl Walker. Wayne Harris. Ben Groß. Yarik Molina. John Wooten. Evelyn Perez. Lathan Andrews. Corby Stephens. Hanani Gladys. Pat Kliever. André Springhut. Daniel Najombong. Josh Porter. Shiza Kancherla. Mark Riley. Shilsha Kancherla. Joseph O'Keefe. Jaine Emiliano. Gabriel Nunes. Letitia Olivier. Andrew Valencia.

Endnotes

1. *Crimewatch* was the British version of the *America's Most Wanted* television series.

2. Katherine Ramsland Ph.D., "Trust Your Gut? Not So Fast", *Psychology Today* (March 2, 2013). https://www.psychologytoday.com/us/blog/shadow-boxing/201303/trust-your-gut-not-so-fast

3. This was in reply to the question posed by Roy Lloyd, a Lutheran minister.

4. John C. Maxwell, *Developing the Leader Within You Workbook*, (Nashville, TN: HarperCollins Leadership, 2001) p. 7.

5. Ariel, just in case you were wondering.

6. Megan Fellman, "Scientists determine four personality types based on new data," *Northwestern Now* (September 17, 2018). Researchers led by Northwestern Engineering's Luis Amaral analyzed data from more than 1.5 million questionnaire respondents that prove four distinct clusters of personality types exist. https://news.northwestern.edu/stories/2018/september/are-you-average-reserved-self-centered-or-a-role-model/

7. Dr. Jordan B. Peterson is a professor and clinical psychologist at the University of Toronto. From the YouTube video "Jordan Peterson - Why The Idea of 'Just Accept Yourself!' is Nihilistic and Insane", Bite-sized Philosophy Channel at timestamp 4:02. Published on Jul 28, 2017. https://www.youtube.com/watch?v=shFbWTEZx_w

8. Travis Bradberry and Jean Greaves, *Emotional Intelligence 2.0* Unabridged Edition (San Diego, CA: TalentSmart, 2009) p. 7.

9. Taken from members of four different Research Groups: for-profit, non-profits, neighborhood, and online. Note that these quotes have occasionally been edited for grammar, clarity, and cohesiveness.

10. Carl Jung, *Psychological Types* (Princeton, NJ: Princeton University Press, 1976) p. 516.

11. A person who always tries to behave well and do the right thing but may try too hard to be perfect.

12. A person who chases an ideal, possibly an unrealistic one, in the hope of realizing a better world.

13. A person who enjoys making clever deals with others in order to reach their goals.

14. A person who works in unlikely ways to save the world, engrossed in their thoughts and ideas to the point of losing track of their surroundings.

15. Defined by *Merriam-Webster's Dictionary* as "one's special trait, interest, or activity."

16. Please note that this is in relation to your personality and not your character.

17. 2 Corinthians 12:10, *The Holy Bible*, New International Version.

18. For Paul the Apostle's original advice, see Hebrews 12:1 contained in *The Holy Bible*.

19. My paraphrase of teaching by John Maxwell in his book, *Developing the Leader Within You* (Nashville, TN: Thomas Nelson, 2000).

20. Ben Healy, "How to Make Friends, According to Science," *The Atlantic* (September 15, 2018), https://www.theatlantic.com/magazine/archive/2018/09/how-to-make-friends/565742/.

21. Alex Ferguson and Michael Moritz, *Leading: Learning from Life and My Years at Manchester United* (New York, NY: Hachette Books, 2016), p. 90.

22. Modern paraphrase of Titus 1:15 taken from the epistle to Titus from Paul the Apostle, *The Holy Bible*.

23. Malcolm Gladwell, *Talking to Strangers: What We Should Know about the People We Don't Know* (New York, NY: Little, Brown and Company, 2019), p. 72.

24. Elizabeth Kolbert, "The Things People Say" *The New Yorker* (October 26, 2009), https://www.newyorker.com/magazine/2009/11/02/the-things-people-say.

25. Fareed Zakaria, "Bile, venom, and lies: How I was trolled on the Internet" *Washington Post* (January 14, 2016), https://www.washingtonpost.com/opinions/bile-venom-and-lies-how-I-was-trolled-on-the-internet/2016/01/14/62207a2c-baf8-11e5-829c-26ffb874a18d_story.html.

26. James, the brother of Jesus, in James 3:4-5 *The Holy Bible*.

27. Dr. Jordan B. Peterson is a professor and clinical psychologist at the University of Toronto. From the YouTube video "Jordan Peterson - Why The Idea of 'Just Accept Yourself!' is Nihilistic and Insane", Bite-sized Philosophy Channel at timestamp 4:02. Published on Jul 28, 2017. https://www.youtube.com/watch?v=shFbWTEZx_w

28. Donald O. Clifton, *Now Discover Your Strengths* (Washington, D.C.: Gallup Press, 2017), page 149.

29. Vinyl music records are produced in two sizes. Single play records rotate at 45 rpm (revolutions per minute), whereas long play (LP) records which hold an entire album rotate at 33 rpm.

30. Lee Colan, "Carnegie's Wisdom on Mining for Gold" *Corp Magazine* (October 6, 2016).

31. 1 Corinthians 15:33, *The Holy Bible*.

32. Paul Scanlon is a mentorship leader who invokes this principle in his teachings. See more info at paulscanlon.com

33. Red blood cells live for about four months, while white blood cells live on average more than a year. Skin cells live about two or three weeks. Colon cells have it rough: They die off after about four days. Sperm cells have a lifespan of only about three days, while brain cells typically last an entire lifetime (neurons in the cerebral cortex, for example, are not replaced when they die). Taken from https://www.livescience.com/33179-does-human-body-replace-cells-seven-years.html

34. A paraphrased proverb of the Jewish king, Solomon, who was renowned for his wisdom. Proverbs 18:15, *The Holy Bible*.

35. Discover this at TheShapesTest.com by making a small donation to the mentoring of young people.

36. Malcolm Gladwell, *Talking to Strangers: What We Should Know about the People We Don't Know* (New York, NY: Little, Brown and Company, 2019).

37. Composed by the American theologian Reinhold Niebuhr sometime in 1932-33.

38. Paul Gibbs, *Kingdom Pioneering: Fulfill God's Calling* (Colleyville, TX: Harris House Publishing, 2017).

39. John Maxwell, "The Law of Magnetism" *The 21 Irrefutable Laws of Leadership* (Nashville, TN: HarperCollins Leadership, 1997), page 103.

40. To discover the order and percentage of your Shape, take the test at TheShapesTest.com, where you can make a donation to our work in schools mentoring teenagers in building healthy relationships.

41. Viv Thomas, *Future Leader: Spirituality, Mentors, Context, and Style for Leaders of the Future* (London, UK: Paternoster Press, 1997).

42. Excerpt taken from the TED talk, *How YouTube is Driving Innovation*, by Chris Anderson, September 14, 2010. https://www.youtube.com/watch?v=X6Zo53M0lcY&vl=en

43. Kurt Lewin, 1926. Wera Mahler, 1933. Peter Gollwitzer, 1982 and 2009.

44. Matthew Powell, CEO of Moroch Advertising Agency, Dallas, Texas, USA.

45. This quote is widely attributed to Mother Teresa, although there does not appear to be a direct source for it.

46. Paul Gibbs, *Shalom: How to Reach Anyone Anywhere* (Colleyville, TX: Harris House Publishing, 2019).

About the Author

Paul Clayton Gibbs is the creator of The Shapes Test. He and his wife, The Foxy Lynn, have two adult sons and have recently become the proud grandparents of two beautiful girls. Originally from Manchester, England, the Gibbs family moved to the USA in 2005.

Founder of The Pais Movement, a faith-based organization that creates workable symmetry between organizations, Paul seeks to help people build something good together. Paul has written several books and spends a significant amount of time traveling throughout the world speaking at conferences, businesses, churches and other acting as a consultant for various networks. His primary topics are leadership development, mentoring and missional living. He is the CEO of The Masterclass Suite and is also the creator of various training 'templates' aimed at 'Mobilizing the many, not just the few.'

Paul enjoys swimming, sailing, bodyboarding, skiing, snowboarding, mountain biking and is a lifelong Manchester United fan!

instagram paulcgibbs
facebook paulclaytongibbs
instagram theshapestest
facebook theshapestest

Made in the USA
Columbia, SC
12 October 2021